A

TREATISE

ON

FIELD FORTIFICATION,

CONTAINING

INSTRUCTIONS ON THE METHODS OF LAYING OUT,
CONSTRUCTING, DEFENDING, AND ATTACKING

INTRENCHMENTS,

WITH THE GENERAL OUTLINES ALSO

OF

THE ARRANGEMENT, THE ATTACK AND DEFENCE

OF

PERMANENT FORTIFICATIONS.

———

BY D. H. MAHAN,

Professor of Military and Civil Engineering in the United States
Military Academy.

———

THIRD EDITION, REVISED AND ENLARGED.

NEW YORK:
JOHN WILEY, 56 WALKER ST.
—
1862

TO
THE OFFICERS OF MILITIA
OF
THE UNITED STATES.

GENTLEMEN:—

THAT an efficiently organized Militia is the firmest and only safe bulwark of the State, is a political axiom admitted by all who understand the nature of our free institutions. Whatever, then, may contribute, in any degree, to strengthen this arm of our national defence, it is to be hoped will meet with an indulgent reception from those to whose province it falls to instruct, discipline, and lead it into action. Feeling a strong conviction that its efficiency must depend upon sound elementary military knowledge, I have presumed to dedicate the following work to you, Gentlemen, in the hope that it may be found useful to our country, by proving serviceable to yourselves. Should this, my chief aim, be accomplished, I shall receive the highest gratification, in being thus enabled to make some return to my country, for the benefit which she has conferred on me in an education at our only National School.

With sentiments of high respect,

I have the honor to be,

GENTLEMEN,

Your obedient servant,

D. H. MAHAN

UNITED STATES' MILITARY ACADEMY,
W r POINT.

NOTICE.

☞ THIS Work will be speedily followed by "INSTRUCTIONS ON OUT-POST AND DETACHMENT DUTIES OF TROOPS," drawn from the latest and most reliable Military Writers, intended for the use of Subaltern and other Officers of Volunteers and Militia.

PREFACE.

In preparing the work now laid before the public, which is chiefly designed for the use of the Cadets of the United States' Military Academy, the aim of the writer was to make a book which should also be generally useful,—one that should contain all the principles and important details of that branch of the *Art of Fortification* of which it specially treats, developed in a manner to be within the comprehension of any person of ordinary intelligence,—a book not for the study alone, but one which the officer can take with him into the camp, and consult at any moment.

With respect to the contents, the writer has collected his information from every source within his reach; rejecting all unnecessary discussions, and admitting no results, which have not either been submitted to a rational analysis, or tested by fair experiment; preferring, in all cases, the views of persons who wrote from their own experience, to the conjectures of others whose theories, however plausible, rested on a less solid foundation.

In arranging the matter, the writer has endeavored, as far as it was practicable, to confine the text to the principles alone, reserving the minor details for the plates, and the explanations appended to them; and on this point he would hazard one or two remarks.

Much that appertains to the Engineer's Art is but an affair of feet and inches; facts which are the results of long usage, holding, in many instances, the important position of principles. His experience has taught him that those authors are the clearest who enter into the minutiæ of their subject; and that with pupils of superior minds, a thorough knowledge of details is an invaluable aid in unravelling the difficulties, and retaining the principles of the Art; whilst, with those of limited capacities, a want of such detail leaves them with the most vague and unsatisfactory notions.

Having said thus much of the plan of the work, a few words, respecting its object, may not be misplaced. The importance of a knowledge of Field Fortification, to officers of all arms in the regular army, need not be insisted upon; the daily occurrences of a campaign demonstrate this too clearly. To the militia officer, this knowledge is even of more importance than to the regular; for called upon, in many cases, to act without the co-operation of regular troops, in the defence of his own fire-side, he will require all those conservative means which add strength and confidence to irregular forces when brought for the first time before an enemy.

To suppose irregular forces capable of coping on equal terms with disciplined troops, is to reason, not only against all probability, but against a vast weight of testimony to the contrary. It is not indeed that discipline confers individual courage; certainly a greater proportion of this essential military virtue will, in all cases, be found among the militia, composed as it must be of men of a higher grade of moral and intellectual qualities, than is to be met with among the common soldiery of any country. But these men, with all the superior advantages that must actuate the volunteer, necessarily want that indispensable element of success, in pitched battles, which results from discipline and habitual training. Called out on a particular emergency, with little or no previous exercise in the services they are required to render, militia cannot have that shoulder-to-shoulder courage, by which men are animated, who have served long together, which begets a reliance on each other, and a confidence in their chiefs, and which is one of the surest guaranties of victory. But place the militia soldier on his natural field of battle, behind a breastwork, and an equilibrium between him and his more disciplined enemy is immediately established; with a feeling of security in his position, his confidence in his own exertions is restored; with a full certainty that his enemy cannot close upon him, before he can retire beyond his reach, he does his duty coolly, and with an execution so terrible, as to have placed the achievements of our militia, from the day of Bunker Hill, to the closing scene of our last war at New Orleans, on a line with the most brilliant military exploits of the best disciplined troops in the world.

But were not these reasons in themselves sufficient, others of greater cogency could be adduced, in favor of intrenched positions for militia. Its ranks are filled with all that is most valuable in society. The farmer, the mechanic, the merchant, the members of the learned professions, must all quit their peaceful avocations to meet the foe. The father of the family jeopards its future prosperity, the son exposes his widowed mother to the chances

of an old age of penury, to bare their breasts to a
mercenary band, without other home, without other
ties, than the camp affords.   Surely nothing but a
reckless disregard for the best interests of society
could urge men, under such circumstances, to
forego the advantages of every possible conservative
means.

The chapters of the work on Military Bridges
Reconnaissances, and Permanent Fortification, are
necessarily incomplete.   A full discussion of these
subjects did not come within the limits of the
writer's plan.   The Military Art, in all its branches,
is founded upon a comprehensive and thorough
knowledge of the exact and physical sciences; and
in no one branch is the importance of this knowledge more felt, than in that of Engineering.   In
adding, therefore, these chapters, a clear comprehension of which supposes an advanced state of
scientific attainment in the reader, it was far from
the writer's intention to lead his fellow citizens into
error, by spreading a knowledge necessarily of a
superficial kind amongst them ; but he rather hopes
it may serve the purpose of fixing their attention
more strongly and minutely upon a profession,
which requires the season of youth to be spent in
thoroughly acquiring its elements, and the devotion
of mature age to an incessant study of its principles, and their applications.

*The author is indebted to Lieut. J. E. BLAKE,
6th* INFANTRY, *for the very correct and handsome
execution of the original drawings, from which the
plates were engraved.*

TABLE OF CONTENTS.

INTRODUCTORY CHAPTER

ON THE EFFECTS OF MUSKETRY AND ARTILLERY

AND THE MEANS OF DIRECTING THEIR FIRE TO OBTAIN THE BEST RESULTS.

As the object of all defensive arrangements, whether artificial objects be raised, or the natural features only of a position be seized upon for the purpose, is to place troops under cover from the enemy's fire, and to enable them to deliver their own with effect, some knowledge of the chances of hitting a mark of given dimensions at various distances, as well as the influences which the undulations and character of the ground, and the physical and mental state of the party firing, may have upon their aim, are essential elements in estimating the advantages which they present. The object of this introductory chapter is to present, from the most recent and authentic sources, some of the facts *arrived at by experiment*, which bear on the question.

I. *Remarks on Target Practice of Small Arms.* There is no fact more striking than the great disproportion between the number of combatants put *hors de combat* and the amount of ammunition expended, even in the most bloody engagements. Hundreds of instances might be cited in support of this. Military writers estimate that not more than one ball out of ten thousand attains its mark; and it is estimated, for example, that in the Expedition of the French to Algiers, in 1830, which lasted but 15 days, upwards of three millions of cartridges were consumed. The causes of this disproportionate application of means to an end, may be found partly in a careless use of his ammunition by the soldier; partly in the want of good instruction and frequent practice, particularly in those men who have not been familiar with the use of fire-arms from their youth; partly in the haste with which a fire against an enemy is delivered, which destroys calmness and good order, and impairs the aim; but chiefly by the over estimation of distance caused by fear, smoke, and the moveable character of the mark.

Much depends upon the attention to his duties paid by the officer to prevent this. The men should be frequently practised at target firing, and be taught to note the influence which the firmness with which the piece is pressed against the shoulder, its depression or elevation, according to the distance of the target and the character of the ground, both as to the hardness of its surface and its undulations, have upon the accuracy of the aim. This practice should not be confined to the open field, but be also extended to the various positions in which soldiers may be placed behind breastworks and other shelters, such as palisades, stoccades, loopholed walls, abattis arranged for defence, &c., in order that the soldier may feel himself perfectly at home under all circumstances, and not be called upon to cast about for the best way of managing his piece in every new emergency. So far from urging the men to load and fire rapidly, every pains should be taken by the officer to impress upon them the necessity of not hurrying, of keeping perfectly cool, o' loading steadily and aiming deliberate.y. Volley firing is admirable practice for this purpose; that by files is apt to give a slovenly and hurried action to the soldier. The fire of troops in line should be kept, as far as possible, under the control of the officer. His position and means of estimating distance enable him far better to judge of the proper moment than the men generally can. It is generally admitted that not more than four or five rounds can be fired in two minutes, allowing the men time to aim deliberately; three may be fired in one minute, but at the expense of a good aim.

As all infantry now are instructed as well in the duties of skirmishers as in the ordinary service of the line, they should be practised at firing both at a small mark, like the ordinary round target, and at a large square one, with black bands made across it, showing the ordinary height of the knees, centre of the body, the breast, shoulders, head and top of the cap.

As the point blank of the musket fired with the bayonet off is at about 120 or 130 yards, to attain a point at this distance, it must be directly aimed at; when it is at a distance short of this the aim must be below it; and when at one over this the aim must be above it. With the bayonet fixed the musket has no point blank, and to hit a point the aim must always be above it.

The following rules for aiming are given by Robert, a recent French author of high standing, in a work on artillery, as drawn from the practice of the French.

To hit the centre of the body, at all distances up to 110 yards, with bayonet fixed, aim at the breast.

To hit the same point, from 110 to 150 yards distance, aim at the shoulders.

To hit the same point, from 150 to 200 yards distance, aim at the head.

To hit the same point, from 200 to 220 yards distance, aim at the top of the cap.

To hit the same point, from 220 to greater distances, aim according to circumstances.

II. *Probable Effects of Small Arms.* Beyond 220 yards the effect of the fire is very uncertain. Beyond 450 yards the ball seldom gives a dangerous wound, although the musket, fired under an elevation of 4°, or 5°, will carry from 600 to 70C yards, and under greater elevations over 1000 yards.

The nature of the surface of the ground, as has already been stated, has considerable influence upon the efficacy of the fire. In broken, or ploughed ground, fire is less effective than on an even firm surface, since in the former the balls that strike it are embedded, whereas in the latter they *ricochet*, and thus attain their mark; it being estimated that, under favorable circumstances, about one-seventh of the balls produce their effect in this way.

Table of effects of fire on a target 5 feet 9 inches high, and 95 feet in length.

No. of balls out of 100 that hit the mark.	Distance to the Target in yards.					
	85	170	255	340	425	510 yds.
On even ground by direct and ricochet shots.	75	50	27	20	14	7
On broken ground by direct shots.	67	38	16	6	3	5
Penetration into pine, &c., in inches at same distances.	3.3 in.	2.2	1.2	0.7	0.4	0.1
Do. into oak same distances.	4 in.	2.3	1.2	0.6	0.4	0.1

In rifle practice with the ordinary rifle, owing to the greater length of time requisite to load this arm, there is some compensation for the more unceitain aim of the musket in short ranges and large targets. When the distance is under 170 yards and the mark large, the effects of the two arms are nearly equal. But for distances of 220 yards, and beyond, the balance is greatly in favor of the rifle. This superiority of the rifle is more particularly observable in the latest improvements of this arm, by Hall, in loading at the breach.

Decker, a German author of reputation, lays down the following, as the probable number of balls out of 100 which will attain their aim, when fired by well instructed troops, making full allowance for the over-estimation of distances in firing on an enemy.

Troops firing in line at	300 paces, out of 100 balls	1 will touch.
" "	200 " "	20 "
" "	100 " "	40 "
" as skirmishers	400 " . "	5 "
" "	300 " "	10 "
" "	200 " "	30 "
" "	100 " "	80 "
Rifle practice	400 " "	10 "
" "	300 " "	90 "
" "	200 " "	72 "

The firing of skirmishers is the more effective from the greater deliberation in aiming and in seizing upon the opportune moment. Volleys produce a tremendous staggering effect, by the simultaneous fall of numbers, when they are coolly thrown in at short ranges. To produce this effect they ought not to be delivered at greater distances than 200 paces.

Decker condemns file firing except for the purpose of occupying new troops when first brought before an enemy.

III. *Ranges and probable effects of Field Artillery.* —In artillery practice, the greatest deliberation and coolness must be exercised to obtain good results. There are so many circumstances which affect the aim of artillery, that nothing but the most careful attention to the effects produced by the first few rounds will enable the officer to manage his guns with advantage.

The point blank range of six pounder field guns is about 600 yards, and that of twelve pounders about 700 yds. The chances of hitting a mark are less with pieces of small than of large calibre, owing to windage, the effect of wind, &c. The ranges of all calibres vary more when the pieces are fired under small angles of elevation than under large angles.

The following Tables of the number of balls out of 100 which will attain a target 6 feet high, and 95 feet in length, at various distances, is taken from Piobert :—

Distances in yards.	550	870	1300
No. of 12 pdr. shot (French) out of 100	57	38	19
" 6 " " " "	49	32	12

Table of the number of balls out of 41 in a canister which attain a butt 6 feet high, and fifty feet in length.

Distances in yards	220	440	660
12 pdr. canister (French)	9	9	4.5
8 " " "	8.3	7.4	4

The usual diameter of grape is about one-third that of the ball. To produce a good effect at a distance, grape ought not to be less than one inch in diameter. Smaller balls produce greatest effects at short distances. Grape of one-third the diameter of the ball has sufficient velocity at 880 yards with 12 pounders, and 760 yards with 8 pounders, to disable men. When the distance is within 500 yards, the fire of grape is superior to that of ball against troops.

In howitzer practice the shells are fired with small charges, as they break easily when they strike an obstacle with a great velocity. The point blank of the howitzer varies with the charge. The greatest range of the twenty-four pdr. howitzer is about 2200 yards; that of the six inch about 2600 yards.

The chances of hitting a mark with the howitzer diminish with the length of the bore, the calibre and weight of the shell. The deviations with small charges are nearly double those with heavy charges.

The shell of the howitzer produces no effect when fired against masonry, as it invariably breaks. It imbeds itself in earth and wood, and bursting produces a considerable crater. The fragments of the shell are often thrown to distances over 600 yards, and they do great damage to objects near. The wounds from them are very dangerous. The shells loaded with incendiary composition are used to fire buildings.

The rate of firing for field guns is from 35″ to 40″ for six pdrs., and one minute for twelve pdrs. But when the enemy is close at hand, and deliberate aim not necessary, two rounds may be fired per minute.

IV. *Selection of positions for field batteries.* The position taken up on the field for a battery must be looked at in a double point of view. 1st, as to its suitableness for annoying the enemy and

2d, as to its being favorable for limiting the effects of the enemy's fire aimed at the battery.

As a general rule artillery should overlook all the ground over which an enemy might advance, the pieces of heaviest calibre being placed on the most commanding points. The batteries, howe er, should not be within musket range of woods, or of any ground where the enemy's sharpshooters might find cover to annoy them. The slope of the ground on which the gun rests must not be too oblique to the line of fire, otherwise the shot will not tell; the declivity of the ground should never exceed one perpendicular to fifteen base. When the ground between the battery and the enemy is horizontal and firm, it will be best to take a position near the enemy, as the ricochet shots on such ground do not rise much. If the ground is uneven a distant position may be more favorable to obtain a grazing fire. Positions should be so chosen that hollows, woods, villages, &c., on the front, or flank of the line occupied by the troops, may be thoroughly swept, to prevent the enemy's columns from approaching under cover.

Advantage should be taken of any unevenness of ground to place the artillery under cover until called into action. But all broken ground occupied by batteries should be thoroughly examined, and the avenues leading to it, by which the enemy's cavalry might fall upon the batteries, should be obstructed. Stony ground is a bad position for a battery, owing to the effect of the enemy's shot in scattering the stones. Very even ground is unfavorable, as well as uneven ground which opens in a funnel shape outwards from the battery, as the enemy is enabled in either case to concentrate his fire from an extended front upon the battery. Rough ground breaks the effects of the enemy's ricochet ɔʌots, and when it presents bluffs or perpendicular faces towards the enemy it will stop the balls that strike those parts. Undulating ground hinders the enemy from observing the effects of his fire. If the ground in rear of the battery is hidden the enemy will generally aim too high; but if the battery is relieved against the sky it will assist his aim. It must be borne in mind that in taking advantage of undulations to cover a battery it will not do to fire from behind the covering ridge, as the aim and range will be rendered very uncertain. Batteries should never be placed directly in front of other troops, since they necessarily attract the enemy's fire to them, and would therefore cause great damage to the troops in rear.

V. *Management of the fire of batteries.* The management of the fire with regard to the projectile to be used is very important. It has been observed that the ball and howitz produce a greater moral effect upon troops than grape. When it is taken into consideration that a six pdr. shot will take off twenty-four ranks at a distance of 500 to 600 yards, the tremendous effect of a smashing fire of ball upon a column may be readily understood. A fire of ball or shells should, therefore, be opened upon troops at a distance, when they are in mass, in several lines, or when an enemy's line can be enfiladed. When an enemy's column is advancing a fire of ball should be opened on the head of the column; and if it be in retreat the aim ought to be directed on the centre. The fire of shells is good against cavalry, as it produces disorder from the explosion of the shell.

A fire of grape or canister should be opened on troops in line, or in open order, but not at distances greater than 600 or 800 yards. In an attack upon troops in line, a battery may advance to within 400 or 500 yards before opening its fire of grape; and even nearer if the ground is unfavorable to ricochet, and there is but little danger from an attack of the enemy's skirmishers on the flanks of the battery When an enemy's battery advances nearer than point blank range, a fire of grape should be opened upon it, just at the moment when having commenced the movement to place the pieces in battery, the flanks of the horses will be offered to the fire.

As a general rule, the aim should be rather low, as ricochet shots produce considerable moral effect. For this purpose, when the ground is favorable to this fire, the aim should be at the mark, but rather under it for distances within 1200 yards; beyond this, and up to 1800 yards, when this fire becomes inefficacious, the piece may be fired with an elevation of one degree between its axis and the ground.

Our fire should be concentrated on several points in succession; but the pieces of the battery should be separated at wide intervals, when the position will admit of it, to offer fewer chances to the divergence of the enemy's shot. It is seldom of any use to fire a single piece at a small mark, as a group of a few individuals; if it be suspected that any important personage may be in such a group we should let them have the discharge of an entire battery at once.

The ammunition of the pieces should be economized, unless it be necessary to drown the fears of new troops in noise.

VI. *Position of Batteries in Attacking and Defending Intrenchments.* In the attack of intrenched positions, the batteries should be placed to obtain

enfilading views on the enemy's lines, and a fire be
opened with ball and shells from pieces of the heaviest calibre. When our column of attack has arrived near the works, the batteries should be so
posted as to support it if repulsed.

In the defence of works, the pieces should be so
placed as to cross their fire upon the ground over
which the enemy must approach. The heaviest
pieces should be placed on the most secure points,
and in such positions that their fire may not incom-
mode the troops defending the work. The light
guns should be placed at the advanced points, as
they can be most easily withdrawn. The howitzers
should occupy points from which hollows, woods,
&c., in advance of the works, can be reached by
their shells.

VII. *Effects, &c., of Batteries for Harbor Defence.*
As very erroneous and vague notions are at present
afloat with respect to the effects of artillery against
shipping and batteries, a statement of some of the
more settled points may not be here misplaced.

Heavy ordnance, from 24 pdr. guns upwards, 8
inch sea-coast howitzers, commonly known as *Paix-
han guns,* and heavy mortars, should alone be used
for harbor defences.

The projectiles of heavy guns, after ricocheting under angles of 4° or 5° on water, lose but little of their
velocity ; the ball, for example, of a 24 pdr., after a
ricochet, preserves sufficient force to pierce the side
of a line-of-battle ship at 600 or 700 yards distance.

The destructive ranges of sea-coast howitzers,
fired with heavy charges, are as high as between
3000 and 4000 yards. Those of heavy mortars are
even greater, and their shells fired under great angles will break through two or three decks of a ship.
Both of these projectiles produce the most destruc-

tive effects when they lodge and explode in timber or between decks.

Batteries, if properly placed, have the two-fold advantage of striking shipping either by a direct aim, or by ricochet; and this does not require, as is generally thought, that the battery should be at the water's edge. When shipping cannot approach nearer to the battery than between 200 and 300 yards, it may be from 50 to 53 feet above the water level and still attain a vessel by ricochet shot, by aiming rather low. To effect this the aim should be so taken that the ball, were it to plunge under the vessel, would pass about as far below the water level as the upper deck is above it. If vessels cannot get nearer than between 400 and 500 yards, then the battery will have the same advantages if placed from 80 to 100 feet above the water level. These advantages of ricochet double the chances of batteries, during a calm, at distances between 200 and 700 yards.

The effect of projectiles upon strong masonry is very gradual. It requires several hours of cool, systematic firing, at very short ranges, to open a useful breach in a well built wall of good stone. The effect of shells, fired against walls of brick even, is absolutely null, as they invariably break, and make but a slight impression upon the wall. A brick arch 3 feet thick, covered with about the same thickness of earth, will sustain, without injury, the shock of the largest shells falling from the greatest heights.

In the fire from shipping upon elevated batteries the advantages from ricochet shots are lost. Even when the battery is low if the ground between it and the water be cut into perpendicular steps, the effects of ricochet will be considerably lessened, as every shot that strikes the face of a step will be stopped.

Batteries have this farther advantage over vessels, that the hull and rigging of the latter present a large vulnerable mark for every gun of the former. To compensate for this ships, can bring a large number of guns to bear on the same point.

When batteries are low, and the water will admit of shipping to approach within musket range, the gunners may be driven from their pieces by a fire from the ship tops. To provide against this, there should be a few light guns on secure points to fire into the tops with grape.

DIRECTIONS TO THE BINDER.

FIELD FORTIFICATION.

CHAPTER I.

NOMENCLATURE AND GENERAL PRINCIPLES.

1. ALL dispositions made to enable an armed force to resist, with advantage, the attack of one superior to it in numbers, belong to the ART OF FORTIFICATION.

2. The means used to strengthen a position, may be either those presented by nature, as precipices, woods, rivers, &c., or those formed by art, as shelters of earth, stone, wood, &c.

3. If the artificial obstacles are of a durable character, and the position is to be permanently occupied, the works receive the name of *Permanent Fortification ;* but when the position is to be occupied only for a short period, or during the operations of a campaign, perishable materials, as earth and wood, are mostly used, and the works are denominated *Temporary* or *Field Fortification.*

4. The general appellation of *Intrenchments* is applied to all field works; and a position strengthened by them, is said to be *Intrenched.*

5. To enable troops to fight with advantage, the intrenchments should shelter them from the enemy's

1

fire; be an obstacle in themselves to the enemy's progress; and afford the assailed the means of using their weapons with effect. To satisfy these essential conditions, the component parts of every intrenchment should consist of a covering mass, or embankment, denominated the *parapet*, to intercept the enemy's missiles, to enable the assailed to use their weapons with effect, and to present an obstacle to the enemy's progress, and of a *ditch*, which, from its position and proximity to the parapet, subserves the double purpose of increasing the obstacle which the enemy must surmount before reaching the assailed, and of furnishing the earth to form the parapet.

6. Intrenchments should be regarded only as accessories to the defence of a position. They are inert masses, which, consuming a portion of the enemy's efforts, and detaining him in an exposed situation to the fire of the assailed, insure his defeat.

7. The general form of a parapet and ditch, to fulfil the above conditions, will be best understood by an examination of the *profile* (Fig. 1), which is a section of the intrenchment made, by a vertical plane, perpendicular to the general direction of the intrenchment.

8. The *exterior slope* is the part of the parapet towards the enemy; it is usually made with the same slope that the earth when first thrown up naturally takes.

The top of the parapet, denominated the *superior slope*, is the line along which the assailed fire on the enemy.

The *interior slope*, sometimes denominated the *breast height*, is the part against which the assailed naturally lean in the act of firing.

The *banquette* is a small terrace on which the soldier stands to deliver his fire; the top of it is denominated the *tread*, and the inclined plane by which it is ascended the *slope*.

The term *crest* is applied to those points of the profile, where a salient angle is formed; and where a re-entering angle is formed by two lines, the term *foot* is applied to the point, in connection with the name of the superior line; thus, *foot of the exterior slope; foot of the interior slope, &c.*

The *berm* is a horizontal space left between the parapet and the ditch, to prevent the earth from yielding.

The slope of the ditch next to the parapet is the *scarp;* the opposite side the *counterscarp.*

The *glacis* is a small mound of earth raised in front of the ditch; it is seldom used in field works, and is therefore not a constituent part of their profile.

8. The profile shows only the outline of an intrenchment in elevation, and by itself is not sufficient to point out the relative bearing of all the parts. A *plan*, or *trace*, which exhibits the direction of the different lines of the parapet, &c., is, in conjunction with the profile, requisite for this purpose.

9. The plan of intrenchments in general should be so arranged as to procure a mutual defence of the parts. To effect this, certain parts are thrown forward towards the enemy, to receive his attack; they are denominated *advanced parts;* other portions, denominated *retired parts,* are withdrawn from the enemy, and protect by their fire the advanced parts. This arrangement naturally indicates that the general outline of the plan must present an angular system; some of the angular points, denomi

nated *salients*, being towards tne enemy and others denominated *re-enterings*, towards the assailed.

10. When such a disposition is made, it is denominated a *flanked disposition;* because the enemy's flank is attained by the fire of the retired parts when he is advancing upon the salients.

11. A flanked disposition is shown in Fig. 2 The advanced parts are denominated *faces;* the re tired parts, which protect the faces, the *flanks;* the retired part connecting the flanks is the *curtain.*

An angle formed by two faces is denominated a *salient angle*, that formed by two retired parts a *re-entering angle;* and one made by a face and the opposite flank, an *angle of defence.*

The line bisecting a salient angle is denominated the *capital;* the distance from a salient to its opposite flank is a *line of defence.*

12. The form of a parapet, and the direction in which a soldier naturally aims in firing over one, are the causes of two of the most important defects of intrenchments. Owing to the form of the parapet and its height, the fire can take effect only at some distance beyond it, so that when the enemy has approached very near the parapet, particularly when he is in the ditch, the fire will pass over his head, unless the flanks are so arranged that their fire will sweep every point of the ditch ; an arrangement of which particular angular systems are alone susceptible. This space, where the enemy can find a shelter, is, generally, in the ditches at the re-entering angles. It is denominated a *dead space*, or *dead angle.*

13. In delivering his fire a soldier usually aims directly to the front, so that the line of fire and the parapet make nearly a right angle with each other. In consequence of this the salients receive no pro-

tection from themselves, and there is an angular space in front of each of them (which is equal to the supplement of the salient angle) that is defended only by the fire of the flanks. This space is denominated a *sector without fire.*

The dead angles, therefore, depend partly on the flanking dispositions, but chiefly on the height of the parapet. The sectors without fire are defects of the plan alone.

14. The attack and defence of intrenchments bear a necessary relation to each other; and it is upon a knowledge of the course pursued by the assailant, that the principles regulating the defence should be founded.

15. An attack is, generally, opened by a fire of the enemy's artillery, whose object is to silence the fire of the intrenchments, and to drive the assailed from the parapet; when this object is attained, a storming party, which usually consists of a detachment of engineer troops, a column of attack, and a reserve, is sent forward, under the fire of the artillery, to the assault. The detachment of engineer troops precedes the column of attack, and removes all obstacles that obstruct its passage into the ditch. The line of march is directed upon a salient, through a sector without fire, and on the prolongation of the capital, as this line is least exposed to the fire of the works.

When the ditch is gained, the party makes its way to a re-entering angle, where, sheltered from the fire of the flanks, the work is entered by the column of attack, either by making a breach in the parapet, or else by means of ladders. The reserve supports the column of attack in case of need; and, if it is driven from the works, covers its retreat.

16. The manner of making the defence is with

1*

artillery, musketry, the bayonet and sorties. The
enemy is attained at a distance by the fire of the
artillery and musketry, whose effect will chiefly depend on the length of time that he is kept exposed
to it by the ditch, and the obstacles in front of it.
The bayonet is resorted to, as soon as the enemy
shows himself on the berm; and sorties are made,
either when any irresolution or confusion is seen in
the enemy's ranks, or at the moment he is repulsed
from the parapet.

It is from this general outline of the attack and
defence, that the following principles, which regulate the plan and profile of intrenchments, are de-
duced.

I.

17. *A flanked disposition should be the basis of the
plan of all intrenchments.*

The flanks sweep with their fire the ground in
front of the faces; remove sectors without fire and
dead angles; cross their fire in front of the salients;
and take the enemy's column in flank.

II.

Every angle of defence should be 90°.

An acute angle of defence exposes the faces to
the fire of the flanks; an obtuse angle leaves a portion of the ground in front of the face undefended.

III.

A line of defence should not exceed 160 *yards.*

A close fire of musketry is more deadly than one
of artillery the musket will kill at distances be-

tween 250 and 300 yards, but its fire is not very
certain beyond 160 yards; moreover, the enemy
should be attained by the musketry before he gains
the salients.

IV.

A salient angle should not be less than 60°.

A salient less than 60° is too weak to withstand
the effects of weather; the interior space which it
encloses is too confined for the manœuvres of the
troops; it forms a large sector without fire in front
of it; the faces of acute salients are, from their
position, more exposed to the enemy's enfilading
fire than when the angle is obtuse.

V.

A strong profile is essential to a vigorous defence.

The rapidity with which a column of attack
approaches, and the short time it remains exposed
to the fire of the work, unless detained by obstacles
in front of the ditch, render its loss, generally, so
trifling as not to check its march, until it arrives at
the crest of the counterscarp. Here, if the ditch is
deep, some delay ensues in entering it, during which
the column is exposed to a warm fire within short
range. When the ditch is entered, a more serious
obstacle remains to be encountered, in the additional
height of the parapet and scarp; and when this
obstacle is overcome, the enemy presents himself in
a fatigued and exhausted state to the bayonets of the
assailed, who have mounted on the top of their
parapet to meet and drive him back into the ditch.

VI.

*The bayonet should be chiefly relied on to repel the
enemy.*

Unless the assailed are determined to meet the
enemy at the point of the bayonet, they must eva
cuate their works so soon as he has entered the
ditch; a longer delay to retreat would be followed
by the most disastrous consequences.

The results of innumerable actions prove that
the defence with the bayonet is the surest method
of repelling the enemy. The assailed, having now
become the assailant, are assisted by that moral
effect which is produced by a change from a defensive to an offensive attitude. They have moreover
the advantages of position and freshness over a
climbing and exhausted enemy.

VII.

Intrenchments should be arranged to facilitate sorties.

A sortie made on the flank of the enemy, at the
moment when his column is either checked by the
fire of the works, or is in a state of disorder when
entering the ditch, will generally prove decisive in
repelling his attack.

This principle, however, is applicable only to en
gagements with large bodies of troops, defending
works open in their rear. A small detachment
should generally rest satisfied with repulsing the
attack; and should not give up the advantages of
their position, by sallying out to engage the enemy
on unequal terms.

VIII.

*Intrenchments should contain a reserve proportional
to their importance.*

The troops engaged in the immediate defence of
the works might be overpowered by reiterated
assaults of the enemy, unless they are supported by
a reserve. The duties of the reserve are to charge
the enemy in any critical moment of disorder, and
to cover the retreat of the troops if driven from the
parapet.

IX.

Intrenchments should be defended to the last extremity.

The chief object of intrenchments is to enable
the assailed to meet the enemy with success; by
first compelling him to approach, under every dis-
advantage of position, and then, when he has been
cut up by the fire of the works, and is exhausted
by his efforts to reach the parapet, to assume the
offensive, and drive him back at the point of the
bayonet. This object can only be attained by defending the works to the last extremity; and unless
attained, intrenchments would serve little other
purpose than to shelter the assailed from the enemy's
fire; for the damage received by the enemy from
the fire of troops who see safety only in retreat, and
not in a courageous effort to repel the assault, will
be necessarily trifling.

This principle leads to the rejection generally of
advanced works thrown up in front of the principal
intrenchments; and to all dispositions of works in
several lines, where the object is to retreat, successively, from one to the other. If an advanced work
is required for the defence of a point, which cannot
be defended by the principal works, it should be

supported by a reserve, and its garrison not be suffered to retreat, until it is in danger of being overpowered : when it should retire under cover of the reserve. As to retreating from one line to another, one of two things must happen ; either the first line must be evacuated, before the enemy enters the ditch, in order that the assailed may gain their second line in safety ; in which case the first line will be of little service : or else, if the assailed wait until the assault is made on the parapet before retreating, the enemy will enter pell-mell with them into the second line, which will thus be of no service.

Troops in action cannot enter into the spirit of fortification on paper. A retreat carries with it all the moral effects of a defeat ; it inspires the assailant ; renders the retreating corps timid ; and impairs the confidence of the troops of the second line in the strength of their own position, when they see the first line carried with such ease. Add to this, the confusion that must ensue among the best disciplined troops, under such circumstances, and the importance attached to the principle will be fully justified.

CHAPTER II.

18. THE ground occupied by a work is denomi
nated the *site*, or *plane of site*.

The *command* is the height of the interior crest
above the site ; and the *relief* is the height of the
same line above the bottom of the ditch.

19. A fire is said to be *direct, slant,* or *enflad-
ing*, according as its direction is perpendicular to,
makes an angle of 30° with, or is on the prolongation of the line at which it is aimed ; when the line
is taken in the rear the fire is denominated a *reverse
fire ;* and when a given space is defended by the
fire from several points crossing over it, the defence
is denominated a *cross fire.*

20. In planning a work the interior crest is regarded as the directing line in regulating the dimensions of the faces, flanks, &c., because this
line shows the column of fire for the defence.
There exists a necessary subordination between the
plan, relief, and command of works, which pre-
vents the dimensions of the one being regulated
independently of the others ; but, without entering
into a close examination of this necessary co-rela-
tion of the parts, it may be stated generally, that
faces should vary between 30 and 80 yards, flanks
between 20 and 40 yards, and curtains should not
be less than twelve times the relief.

21. A great variety of figures has been used for
the plan of simple intrenchments. They may all
be reduced to the following, the *Right Line ;* the

Redan; the *Lunette,* or *Detached Bastion;* the *Crémaillère,* or *Indented Line;* the *Priest-Cap,* or *Swallow-Tail;* the *Redoubt;* the *Star Fort;* and he *Bastion Fort.*

22. The redan (Fig. 3) is a work consisting of two faces; the *gorge,* or entrance in the rear, being open. This work is used to cover a point in its rear; such as a bridge, defile, ford, &c. Having no flank defences its salient is unprotected, and to obtain a fire in the direction of its capital a short face, denominated a *pan coupé,* is sometimes made in its salient angle.

23. The lunette (Fig. 4) consists of two faces and two flanks. This work is used for the same purposes as the preceding. It has the same defects; but possesses the advantages of sweeping with the fire of its flanks ground which might be badly defended by its faces.

24. The indented line (Fig. 5) serves to convert the direct fire of a right line into a flank and cross fire, and is therefore frequently substituted for the right line.

25. The priest-cap (Fig. 6) is seldom used as a detached work; but is generally combined with the right line and the indented line to procure a flank, or cross fire, in front of them.

26. Any enclosed work of a polygonal form, without re-entering angles, is denominated a redoubt. This work is used to fortify a position which can be attacked on all sides; the works which have already been described, being unsuitable for this purpose, as their gorges are open, and therefore require to be supported by troops, or works, in their rear; except when they are so situated that an attack cannot be made at the gorge.

The square (Fig. 7) is the most common form for a redoubt, on account of the ease with which it is constructed, and the advantage it possesses, when combined with several others, of protecting tne spaces between them by a cross fire.

All redoubts have the same defects. The ditches are unprotected, and there is a sector without fire in front of each salient. For the purpose of remedying the sector without fire, it has been proposed to convert a portion of each face at the salient angles, into an indented line, to procure a fire in the direction of the capitals. This method is not of practical application; and if it could be applied would only serve the purpose of changing the position of the sectors without fire from the salients to other points.

27. The star fort takes its name from the form of the polygonal figure of its plan. (Figs. 8, 9, 10 11.) It is an enclosed work, with salient and re-entering angles; the object of this arrangement being to remedy the defects observed in redoubts. This, however, is only partially effected in the star fort: for, if the polygon is a regular figure, it will be found, that, except in the case of a fort with eight salients, the fire of the faces does not protect the salients; and that in all cases there are dead angles at all the re-enterings. The star fort has, moreover, the essential defect, that occupying the same space as a redoubt, its interior capacity will be much less, and the length of its interior crest much greater, than in the redoubt: it will, therefore, require more men than the redoubt for its defence, whilst the interior space required for their accommodation is diminished. These defects, together with the time and labor required to throw up such a work, have led engineers to proscribe it,

2

except in cases where they are compelled by the
nature of the site to resort to it.

To plan a star fort, its salients should not be
less than 60°, and its faces may vary from 30 to 60
yards.

28. The bastion fort satisfies more fully the con
ditions of a good defence, than any other work; but,
owing to the time and labor required for its construction, it should be applied only to sites of great
importance, which demand the presence of troops
during the operations of a campaign.

The bastion of a fort may consist of a polygon
of any number of sides; but for field forts, the
square and pentagon are generally preferred, owing
to the labor and construction. To plan a work of
this kind, a square or pentagon (Fig. 12) is laid out,
and the sides bisected by perpendiculars; a distance
of one eighth of the side is set off on the perpendiculars in the square, or one seventh in the pentagon; from the angular points of the polygon, lines
are drawn through the points thus set off; these
lines give the direction of the lines of defence;
from the salients of the polygon distances, equal to
two sevenths of the side, are set off on the direction of the line of defence, which give the faces;
from the extremity of the faces, the flanks are
drawn perpendicular to the lines of defence; the
extremities of the flanks are connected by the curtains.

The side of the polygon is termed the *exterior
side*; the line bisecting it, the *perpendicular*; the
angle at the salient is the *flanked angle*; the one
formed by a face and flank, the *shoulder angle*; the
one between the flank and cur'ain, the *angle of the
curtain*; the portion of the work included between
the capitals of two adjacent bastions is denominated
a *bastioned front*, or simply a *front*.

An examination of the arrangement of a bastioned front will show that there are neither dead angles nor sectors without fire; that the salients, and all the ground within the range of musketry, are protected by formidable columns of direct, flank, and cross fire. There is one point in this system that demands particular attention, which is, that the counterscarp of the ditch, if laid out parallel to the interior crest, would form a dead angle along each face near the shoulder; because the fire of the flank would be intercepted by the crest of the counterscarp. To prevent this, either the counterscarps of the faces must be prolonged to intersect, and all earth between them and the scarp of the flanks and curtain be excavated (Fig. 13), or the ditch of each face must be inclined up in a slope from the bottom, opposite the shoulder (Fig. 14), so that it can be swept by the fire of the flank.

The first method is the best, but requires most labor; the second is chiefly objectionable as it gives an easy access to the ditch, which might be taken advantage of in an assault. It is proposed, to obviate this, to dig a second ditch at the foot of the slope across the main ditch, twelve feet wide, and about six feet deep; to make it pointed at the bottom, and to plant a row of palisades in it. The profile through the flank (Fig. 14) shows this arrangement.

Forts have been proposed with half bastions, but, being very little superior to the redoubt, and much more difficult of construction, they ought never to be used.

The exterior sides of the bastion fort should not exceed 250 yards, nor be less than 125 yards, otherwise the flanking arrangements will be imperfect. With a relief of 24 feet, which is the greatest that, in most cases, can be given to field works, and as exterior side of 250 yards, the ditch of the curtain will be perfectly swept by the fire of the flanks, the lines of defence will be nearly 180 yards, a length which admits of a good defence, and the flanks will be nearly 30 yards. With a relief of 14 feet, the least that will present a tolerable obstacle to an assault, and an exterior side of 125 yards, the ditch of the curtain will be well flanked, the flanks will be nearly 20 yards in length, and the faces between 30 and 40 yards. Between these limits, the dimensions of the exterior side must vary with the relief.

29. The defence of enclosed works demands that every point of the parapet should be guarded, at the moment of assault, either by cannon or musketry. The troops may be drawn up for the defence either iu one, two, or three ranks; and there should, moreover, be a reserve proportioned to the importance attached to the work. The free interior space, denominated the *terre-parade plein*, should be sufficiently great to lodge the troops, with the cannon and its accessories, and will therefore depend on the nature of the defence. The following data will suffice to regulate this point.

Each man will occupy one yard, linear measure, along the interior crest, and each cannon from five to six yards. The space requisite to lodge each man is one and a half square yards; and about sixty square yards should be allowed for each gun. Besides this space an allowance must be made for the *traverses*, which are mounds of earth thrown up in the work to cover an outlet, to screen the troops from a reverse, or an enfilading fire, &c.; and for powder magazines, when they are not placed in the traverses. The area occupied by a traverse will depend on its dimensions, and cannot be fixed be-

forehand; that allowed for a magazine for three or
four cannon may be estimated at fifteen or twenty
square yards.

30. As a field fort must rely entirely on its own
strength, it should be constructed with such care
that the enemy will be forced to abandon an attempt
to storm it, and be obliged to resort to the method
of regular approaches used in the attack of permanent works. To effect this, all the ground around
the fort, within the range of cannon, should offer
no shelter to the enemy from its fire; the ditches
should be flanked throughout; and the relief be so
great as to preclude any attempt at scaling the
work.

CHAPTER III.

.

31. The general form of the parapet is the same for all works. Its dimensions will vary with the kind of soil used in its construction; with the time and means that can be employed; with the time that the work is to remain occupied; and, finally, with the time and means that the enemy can dispose of in the attack, and the degree of resistance that the work should offer.

32. The command of the interior crest (Fig. 1.) should be regulated so as to intercept the enemy's missiles, and to shelter the assailed. Men of the greatest ordinary stature, in bringing their muskets to an aim, do not fire at a higher level than about five feet; therefore any mass of this height in front of them will just intercept their fire; but this mass would not shelter a man standing behind it; to effect this, in the case of the tallest men usually found in the ranks, the interior crest should be at least six feet six inches above the terre-parade-plein. The command must then be regulated by these two facts, and this principle may be laid down. *The command of a field work over the ground occupied by the enemy must never be less than five feet; nor less than six feet six inches over that occupied by the assailed.*

But this minimum command would give the assailed only a slight advantage, as the men, when on the banquette, would be still much exposed; and in an assault the height of the parapet would present an inconsiderable obstacle. These defects of low works have led engineers to adopt eight feet the least height of parapet which will admit of respectable defence. The greatest height has beet fixed at twelve feet, owing to the difficulty of throwing up a work with the ordinary means at hand, which are usually only the pick and shovel.

The thickness of the parapet, which is always estimated by the horizontal distance between the interior and exterior crests, is regulated by the material used for the parapet; the kind of attack, and its probable duration.

PENETRATION INTO WELL-RAMMED EARTH COMPOSED OF HALF SAND AND HALF CLAY.

18 pounder,	. .	110 yards	. .	6 feet 6 in.
18 "	. .	440 "	. .	5 " 6 "
18 "	. .	880 "	. .	4 " 6 "
9 "	. .	110 "	. .	4 " 4 "
9 "	. .	440 "	. .	3 " 4 "
9 "	. .	880 "	. .	2 " 8 "
6 inch howitzer,	. .	110 "	charge 3·3 lbs.	4 " 0 "
6 " "	. .	440 "	" "	3 " 0 "
6 " "	. .	880 "	" "	2 " 0 "
24 pounder "	. .	110 "	" 2·2 lbs.	3 " 5 "
24 "	. .	440 "	" "	2 " 5 "
24 "	. .	880 "	" "	1 " 6 "

The penetrations into sand mixed with gravel were about 0·8 of the above; into earth mixed with sand and gravel, about 0·9; into compact soil of clay, sand and mould, 1·1; into common soil, loosely thrown up, about twice the above.

PENETRATION OF MUSKET BALLS.

					inches.
Charge 154 grains, at 34 yards, in oak,	. . . .	3½
" " " 60 " "	. . . .	3
" " " 110 " "	. . . .	2¾
" " " 220 " "	. . . .	1½
" 134 " 50 " "	. . . .	1½
" 154 " 30 " rammed earth, of clay & sand,	10
" " " 60 " " " " " "	9½
" " " 110 " " " " " "	8½
" " " 220 " " " " " "	6
" " " 24 " bundle of fascines, . .	24
" " " 40 " packed wool of matrasses,	40

In order to insure perfect security, the thickness of parapets ought to be one-half greater than the depth of penetration furnished by experiment.

As a general rule, the following dimensions may be taken for the parapets and other coverings for field-works :—

Brick wall of one brick, . . .	
Stone ditto, 6 inches, . . .	
White Pine fence, 12 inches, . .	
Yellow ditto, 9 " . .	Musket proof.
Oak (seasoned), 4 " . .	
Earth, three to four feet, . .	
Earthen parapet against field-pieces, from 9 to 12 feet.	

From experiments carefully made to ascertain the distance into which shot will penetrate the media in most common use for forming parapets, the following results have been obtained :

PENETRATION INTO ROUGH GOOD LIMESTONE MASONRY, WITH A CHARGE ONE-THIRD THE WEIGHT OF THE BALL.

18 pounder shot at about 30 yards,	.			1 foot 9 inches.
18 " " " 110 "	.	.	1 " 8 "
18 " " " 330 "	.	.	1 " 4 "
18 " " " 660 "	.	.	1 " 0 "
9 " " " 30 "	.	.	1 " 4 "
9 " " " 100 "	.	.	1 " 3 " .
9 " " " 330 "	.	.	1 " 0 "
9 " " " 660 "	.	.	0 " 7 "

By adding three-fourths of the above distances to themselves, the penetration into good brick masonry will be obtained.

The effect of shells fired against masonry is very trifling; they either break without exploding, or produce but a slight impression when they explode in contact with the masonry.

PENETRATION INTO OAK WOOD WITH SAME CHARGE.

18 pounder shot, at about 440 yards,	.	.	.	3 ft. 0 in.
18 " " " 880 "	.	.	.	2 " 0 "
9 " " " 440 "	.	.	.	2 " 0 "
9 " " " 880 "	.	.	.	1 " 0 "
6 inch howitzer, " 440 "	charge 3·3 lbs.	1 " 8 "
6 " " " 880 "	" "	1 " 0 "
24 pounder howitzer, " 440 "	" 2·2 lbs.	1 " 3 "
24 " " " 880 "	" "	8 " 0 "

The penetration into white pine is about three-fourths greater than into oak.

34. The superior slope is arranged to defend the crest of the counterscarp; to effect which the fire should not strike below the crest, nor pass more than three feet over it; otherwise, either the counterscarp would be damaged, or the assailed by stooping when near the crest would find a shelter. The inclination of the superior slope, however, should not be greater than one-fourth, nor less than one-sixth, that is, the base of the slope should be between four and six times the height. If greater than one-fourth, it would make the portion of the parapet, about the interior crest, too weak; and if less than one-sixth, the ground directly in front of the work would not be so well defended; moreover, as artillery cannot be fired at a greater depression than one-sixth, without injuring the carriage, this inclination of the superior slope serves as a check in rapid firing.

If, owing to the command, the fire should pass higher than three feet above the crest of the counterscarp, it would then be necessary to construct a glacis in front of the ditch. It must be so arranged that it can be swept by the fire of the work, and be commanded by it at least five feet.

35. The exterior slope is the same that the earth naturally assumes. Any means used to make it steeper would be injurious; because they would be soon destroyed by the enemy's fire, and the earth giving way, the necessary thickness of the parapet would be diminished.

36. The interior slope receives a base equal to one-third its height. This is a result of experience, which has shown that it is the most convenient for the soldier in leaning forward to deliver his fire over a parapet.

37. The tread of the banquette is placed four feet

three inches below the interior crest; this will ad
mit men of the lowest ordinary stature, to fire con-
veniently over the parapet. Its width is two feet
for a defence with one rank; and four feet for two
or three ranks; because the third rank does not
fire, and is therefore placed on the banquette slope,
the base of which is twice the altitude, to render
the ascent convenient. When the tread of the banquette is very high, and particularly in enclosed
works, where interior space is wanted, steps may be
substituted for a slope; the rise of the step should
be nine inches, and its breadth twelve inches. The
tread of the banquette should receive a slope of two
inches to the rear to drain off the surface water.

38. The berm is a defect in field works, because
it yields the enemy a foot-hold to breathe a moment,
before attempting to ascend the exterior slope. It
is useful in the construction of the work for the
workmen to stand on; and it throws the weight of
the parapet back from the scarp, which might be
crushed out by this pressure. In firm soils, the
berm may be only from eighteen inches to two feet
wide; in other cases, as in marshy soils, it may require a width of six feet. In all cases, it should be
six feet below the exterior crest; to prevent the enemy, should he form on it, from firing on the troops
on the banquette.

39. The ditch should be regulated to furnish the
earth for the parapet. To determine its dimensions,
the following points require attention; its depth
should not be less than six feet, and its width less
than twenty feet, to present a respectable obstacle
to the enemy. It cannot, with convenience, be
made deeper than twelve feet; and its greatest
width is regulated by the inclination of the superior

slope, which, produced, should not pass below the crest of the counterscarp.

40. The slopes of the scarp and counterscarp will depend on the nature of the soil, and the action on it of frost and rain. The scarp is less steep than the counterscarp; because it has to sustain the weight of the parapet. It is usual to give the slope of the scarp, a base equal to two-thirds of the base of the natural slope of a mound of fresh earth whose altitude is equal to the depth of the ditch; the base of the counterscarp slope is made equal to one half the same base.

41. To determine the exact dimensions of the ditch, for a given parapet, requires a mathematical calculation, which will be given in a Note. On the field a result may be obtained, approximating sufficiently near the truth for practice, by assuming the depth of the ditch and dividing the surface of the profile of the parapet by it to obtain the width. In excavating the ditch it will be found that more earth will be furnished at the salients than is required there for the parapet; and that the re-enterings will not always furnish enough. On this account, the width of the ditch should not be uniform, but narrower at the salients than the re-enterings.

CHAPTER IV.

MANNER OF REGULATING THE RELIEF OF INTRENCH-MENTS ON IRREGULAR SITES.

42. When a work is placed on level ground, it usually receives a uniform relief; but when the site is irregular, or there are commanding eminences within cannon range, a uniformity of relief cannot be preserved, because it might expose the interior of the work to the enemy's view, from the commanding points.

43. The plan will also be modified by the same causes. The principal faces should so be placed as not only to guard all the points where an enemy might approach; but the enemy should not be able to take up their prolongations to obtain an enfilading, or a reverse fire upon them. The position of the points to be guarded, and that of the commanding eminences, require to be carefully studied, before adopting any definitive plan. The only general rules that can be laid down, are to lay out the principal lines so as to obtain a direct and cross fire, on the approaches of the enemy; and placing them, at the same time, as nearly parallel as practicable, to the general direction of the crests of the commanding heights, in order that the enemy occupying the crest may have a direct fire alone on these parts.

44. When the enemy occupies a position more elevated than the work, he is said to have a *plunging fire* on it; and when the relief of the work is so regulated as to intercept this fire, the work is said to be *defiled*.

45. The *defilement* of field works is not indis-

pensable to a good defence, nor is it generally
practicable. It is, however, not only a conservative
means, but it also inspires the assailed with confidence; for the soldier regards with distrust the
strength of his position, when he finds himself
exposed to the view of the enemy from an elevated
point.

44. The defilement of a work is a practical
operation performed on the ground in the following
manner :—

Let A B C D E (Fig. 15) be the plan of a work,
a lunette for example; and the points o, o, &c., the
most elevated points of a commanding position in
front of the work. At the points A, B, &c., let
straight poles be planted vertically, and on the poles
along the gorge line let a point be marked, at three
feet above the ground. Let two pickets be driven
in the ground along the gorge line, and a cord a, b,
or a straight edge of pine, be fastened to them, on
the same level as the two points marked on the
poles at A and E. Let an observer now place himself in the rear of a b, so as to bring the poles at
B, C, and D, and the points o, o, &c., within the
same field of vision. Let observers be placed at B,
C, and D. The first observer now sights along a b,
until he brings his eye in the position that a b will
appear tangent to the most elevated of the points o.
Having accurately determined this position, he next
directs the other observers to slide their hands along
the poles until they are brought into the same plane
of vision with the point o, and the line a b, and to
mark those points on the poles. These points, together with the two first marked, will evidently be
in the same plane, and this plane, produced, will be
tangent to the highest point o. It is denominated
the *Rampant Plane.* Now if a point be marked on

3

each pole, at five feet above the points thus deter
mined; these points will be contained in a second
ideal plane, parallel to the first, and five feet above
it. This plane is denominated the *Plane of Defilement*, and the interior crests of the work are contained in this plane, being the lines joining the
highest points marked on the poles.

As the gorge line is farthest from the heights, and
the rampant plane ascends towards them, it will necessarily pass at more than three feet above every
other point of the parade of the work; and the
plane of defilement, in like manner, will pass at
eight feet above the parade at the gorge, and at five
feet above the highest point o. A plane of defilement is therefore defined to be, *that plane which,
containing the interior crests of a work, passes at
least eight feet above every point of the parade, and
at least five feet above every point that the enemy can
occupy within the range of cannon*, which range may
be taken, with safety, at one thousand yards.

45. When a work is placed in a hollow formed
by two eminences, and is exposed to both a direct
and reverse fire from them, it cannot be defiled by
the means just explained, without giving it a relief
generally too great for field works. To avoid this
the method of reverse defilement must be resorted
to.

46. Let A B C D E (Fig. 16) be the plan of a lunette, placed between the two eminences o, o'; its
face and flank A B C being exposed to the direct fire
from o, and a reverse fire from o'; the other face
and flank being in like manner exposed to a direct
and a reverse fire.

47. Suppose a section of the work (Fig. 17) to
be made by a vertical plane, passing through the
highest points o and o'. If in this plane a vertical,

a b, be drawn, corresponding to the capital of the
work, and eight feet be set off on this vertical from
the point *a*, and two verticals be drawn through the
points o and o', and five feet be set off on each of
them; and then the points *c* and *c'* be joined with
d, it is obvious that the interior crest of the parapet
A, being placed on the line *c d*, will screen all the
ground in the rear of it, as far as the capital, from
the direct fire from o. The parapet B being regulated in a similar manner, will screen all the ground
behind it as far as the same line. But the fire from
o' would take the parapet A in reverse, and that
from o the parapet B; to prevent this, a covering
mass, denominated a *traverse*, must be erected on
the line of the capital, and a sufficient height be
given to it to screen both A and B from a reverse
fire. To effect this, let eighteen inches be set off
above the interior crests of A and B; the point *e*
being joined with *c'*, and the point *e'* with *c*; it is
here also obvious, that if the top of the traverse be
placed on the line *c e'*, it will effectually screen both
the parapets from all reverse fire; because every
shot that strikes the top of it will pass at least
eighteen inches above the two parapets, and, since
the banquettes are four feet three inches below the
interior crests, the shot must pass five feet nine
inches above the banquettes, which will be quite
sufficient to clear the heads of the men when on the
banquettes. This illustration explains the spirit of
the method of reverse defilement. The operation
itself is performed in the following manner.

48. Poles (Fig. 16) are planted at the points
A B C, &c., and one at the point F, where the lines
of the capital and gorge intersect. On the pole
F, a point is marked three feet above the ground,
and a point is likewise marked on the pole at C,

which should be one foot six inches higher than that on F; that is, if the ground between the two poles be level, the point on C will be four feet six inches above the ground. Two stout pickets may next be planted between F and C, and a cord, or a straight edge, be fastened to them, so as to be in the same line as the points marked on the poles.

Observers are then placed at the poles A and B; and another places himself behind the cord so as to bring the posts O, A, and B, in the field of vision with it; then shifting the position of the eye until the cord is brought tangent to the highest point on O, he directs the observers at A and B, to mark on the respective poles the points where the plane of vision intersects them. This operation will determine the rampant plane for one half the work A B C F, that for the other half will be determined by a similar process. If then a distance of five feet be set off on each pole above the points thus determined, these points will fix the position of the interior crests.

It is obvious that the interior crest of the part A B C is not in the same plane as that of the part C D E. These two planes are denominated *planes of direct defilement*.

49. To determine the height of the traverse is the next step. To do this, the height of the tread of the banquette is ascertained on the three poles, B, C, D, and a distance of nine inches is set off on each pole above the tread. Between the points thus determined a cord is stretched, or if the distance be too great for this, two pickets may be placed between B and C, and a cord, or straight edge, be fastened to them in the required direction. An observer is then placed at the pole F, and

another places himself behind the line B C, so as to bring the cord, and the points o' and F, in the field of vision; he then shifts the position of the eye until the cord is brought to touch the point o'; he then directs the observer at F to mark the point on the pole where it is intersected by the plane of vision. A similar operation is performed with the point o, and the face c D, and above the highest point thus determined on F, a distance of five feet is set off for the top of the traverse at F; and five feet nine inches is set off above the tread of the banquette at c for the top of the traverse at that point.

The planes which determine the top of the traverse, are termed *planes of reverse defilement*.

50. The traverse is finished on top like the roof of a house, with a slight pitch; its thickness at top should seldom exceed ten feet, and will be regulated by the means the enemy can bring to the attack; its sides are made with the natural slope of the earth; but, when the height of the traverse is considerable, the base of the side slopes would occupy a large portion of the interior space; to remedy this, in some measure, the portion of the sides which are below the planes of direct defilement, may be made steeper than the natural slope; the earth being retained by a facing of sods, &c.

51. When the salient of the work is arranged for defence, the traverse cannot be extended to the salient angle; it is usual to change its direction within some yards of the salient, and unite it with the face most exposed. Traverses are also used to cover faces exposed to an enfilade fire; for this purpose they are placed perpendicular to the face to be covered. If several are required, they may be placed twenty or thirty yards apart; each traverse

3*

should be about twenty-four feet long, and thick enough to be cannon proof.

52. The cases of defilement here examined, are those of works open at the gorge; the same principles, and similar methods, would be applied to enclosed works. After the plan of the work has been regulated, the arrangement of the traverses next demands the attention; the only rule that can be laid down is, to place them in the most favorable position to intercept the reverse and enfilading fire of the enemy; and if there should be a choice with respect to several positions, to select the one which will give the lowest traverse.

53. The difficulty of defilement, owing to the great relief that may be required for the parapets, the labor of erecting the traverses, and the room which they occupy within the work, which is frequently wanted for the defence, restricts its application mostly to enclosed works, which are to remain occupied during some time, and whose position, from some point to be defended, cannot be shifted.

54. If it is not even probable that a commanding eminence will be occupied by the enemy, nevertheless should the defence be not impaired, it will be better to place the work beyond the cannon range of the eminence.

55. The irregularity in the profile of the parapet, caused by defilement, will occasion a correspondent irregularity in that of the ditch. Where the parapet is highest, the ditch will require to be widest and deepest; for, in order to avoid the removal of the earth to considerable distances, it is best that the earth for each portion of the parapet should be taken from the ditch in front of it. No other rule can be laid down in this case, than to keep the di

mensions of the ditch within the prescribed limits ; and, if this will not admit of its counterscarp being well defended, to raise a glacis in front of it, subject to the fire of the work.

CHAPTER V.

56. THE foregoing chapters contain all that is requisite to determine the plan and relief of field works under all circumstances of variety of ground. To follow a natural order, the next steps will be to describe the manner of laying the work out on the field, which is termed *profiling;* the distribution of the workmen to excavate the ditch, and form the parapet; and the precautions to be observed in the construction.

57. Poles (Fig. 18) having been planted at the angles of the work, and the height of the interior crest marked on them, a line is traced on the ground, with a pick, showing the direction of the interior crests. At suitable distances, say from twenty to thirty yards apart, cords are stretched between two stout pickets, in a direction perpendicular to the line marked out by the pick; these cords should be exactly horizontal. A stout square picket is driven firmly into the ground, where the cord crosses above the pick-line, and a slip of pine, on which the height of the interior crest is marked, is nailed to the picket. The thickness of the parapet is measured on the cord, and a picket driven into the ground to mark the point. The base of the interior slope, and the tread of the banquette, are set off in a similar manner; and a slip of deal is nailed to each of the pickets. The height of the interior crest, and the tread of the banquette, are easily ascertained, from the position of the cord, and the

interior crest; these points having been marked on
their respective slips, the outline of the parapet is
shown by connecting them by other slips, which
are nailed to the uprights; the banquette slope, and
exterior slope, will be determined by a similar
process.

58. From the profiles thus formed perpendicular
to the interior crests, the oblique profiles at the
angles can readily be set up, by a process which
will suggest itself without explanation.

59. Having completed the profiling, the foot of
the banquette, and that of the exterior slope, are
marked out with the pick, and also the crests of the
scarp and counterscarp. All the arrangements preparatory to commencing the excavation are now
complete.

60. Experience has shown that, in ordinary soils,
a man with a pick can furnish employment to two
men with shovels; that, not to be in each other's
way, the men should be from four-and-a-half to six
feet apart; and, finally, that a shovel full of earth
can be pitched by a man twelve feet in a horizontal
direction, or six feet in a vertical direction.

61. To distribute the workmen, the counterscarp
crest is divided off into lengths of twelve feet, and
the interior crest into lengths of nine feet. These
points might be marked out by pickets numbered
one, two, three, &c. In each area, thus marked out,
a working party is arranged consisting of a pick
with two shovels placed near the counterscarp, two
shovels near the scarp, and one man to spread, and
one to ram the earth, for two working parties.

62. The pick commences by breaking ground so
far from the counterscarp crest (Fig. 19) that, by
digging vertically three feet, he will arrive at the
position of the counterscarp. The excavation is

carried on at the same depth of three feet, advancing towards the scarp, where the same precaution is observed as at the counterscarp. The earth is thrown forward, and evenly spread and rammed, in layers of about twelve inches, from the banquette slope to the exterior slope.

63. For the facility of entering the ditch, whilst working, the offsets, at the scarp and counterscarp, may be formed into steps with a rise of eighteen inches each; and, if the ditch is deeper than six feet, an offset, about four feet broad, should be left at the scarp, about mid-depth of the ditch, to place a relay of shovels to throw the earth on the berm. In some cases, a scaffold of plank is raised in the ditch for the same purpose.

64. When the ditch has been excavated to the bottom, the offsets are cut away, and the proper slopes given to the sides. The earth furnished by the offsets, if not required to complete the parapet, may be formed into a small glacis.

65. If the soil is stony, the vegetable mould on the surface should be scraped off, and reserved to form the top of the parapet, which should be made of earth of this kind, to the depth of at least eighteen inches, to prevent injury to the troops from the effect of a shot striking the top, and scattering the pebbles in their faces.

66. In making the parapet, care should be taken to form a drain, at some suitable point, to carry off the water from the interior into the ditch. The water from the drain should not be suffered to run down the scarp, as it would soon destroy it. A gutter, formed of boards, should be made to prevent this.

67. The time required to throw up a work will depend on the nature of the soil and the expertness

of the laborers. From troops unaccustomed to the use of ditching tools, six cubic yards may be considered a fair day's work in ordinary soils, when the earth is not thrown higher than six feet; but when a relay is placed on an offset in the ditch, from four to five cubic yards may be taken as the result of a day's work for each man. Expert workmen will throw up from eight to ten cubic yards at task work.

CHAPTER VI.

68. A *revetment* consists of a facing of stone, wood, sods, or any other material, to sustain an embankment, when it receives a slope steeper than the natural slope.

69. In field works revetments are used only for the interior slope of the parapet and for the scarp; for the first sods, pisa, fascines, hurdles, gabions and plank, are chiefly used; and for the last, timber.

70. *Revetment of sods.* Sod work forms a strong and durable revetment. The sods should be cut from a well-clothed sward, with the grass of a fine short blade, and thickly matted roots. If the grass is long, it should be mowed before the sod is cut.

Sods are of two sizes (Fig. 20), one termed *stretchers*, are twelve inches square, and four-and-a-half inches thick; the others, termed *headers*, are eighteen inches long, twelve inches broad, and four-and-a-half inches thick.

71. The sod revetment (Fig. 21) is commenced as soon as the parapet is raised to the level of the read of the banquette. A course of sods is then aid, either horizontal or a little inclined from the banquette; the course consists of two stretchers and one header alternating, the end of the header laid to the front. The grass side is laid downward; and the sods should protrude a little beyond the line of the interior slope, for the purpose of trimming the course even at top, before laying another, and to make the interior slope regular. The course is

firmly settled, by tapping each sod as it is laid with a spade or a wooden mallet; and the earth of the parapet is packed closely behind the course.

A second course is laid on the first, so as to cover the joints, or, as it is termed, to *break joints* with it; using otherwise the same precautions as with the first. The top course is laid with the grass up; and in some cases pegs are driven through the sods of two courses to connect the whole more firmly, which is, however, by no means necessary to form a strong sodding.

72. When cut from a wet soil, the sods should not be lain until they are partially dried otherwise they will shrink, and the revetment will crack in drying. In hot weather the revetment should be watered frequently, until the grass puts forth. The sods are cut rather larger than required for use; and are trimmed to a proper size from a model sod.

73. *Pisa revetment.* Ordinary earth, if mixed with a proper proportion of clay, and the whole well kneaded with just water enough to cause the particles to adhere when squeezed in the hand, may be used for a revetment, and is termed a pisa revetment. Sometimes chopped straw is mixed up with the mass to cause it to bind better.

74. The pisa is laid in layers of twelve inches thick, and two feet broad, and well packed. The same precautions should be taken in forming the parapet behind it as in sod revetments. The face of the revetment may be sown with grass seed or oats, and when the stalk comes to maturity it should not be cut, but suffered to remain as a kind of thatch to protect the facing from the weather.

75. *Fascine revetment. A fascine* (Fig. 32) is a bundle of twigs closely bound up. There are two

4

sizes of fascines; one size is nine inches in diameter, and about ten feet long; the other, which is generally termed a *soucisson*, is twelve inches in diameter and twenty feet long; it is chiefly used for the revetments of batteries.

76. To make a fascine, straight twigs are selected, between the thickness of the little finger and thumb, the longer the better; they should be stripped of the smaller twigs. A machine, termed a *fascine horse*, is put up, by driving two stout poles obliquely into the ground about two feet, so as to cross each other about two feet above the ground, where they are firmly tied together; as many of these supports as may be required are put up in a straight line, about eighteen inches apart; this forms the horse on which the twigs are laid to be bound together.

77. Another machine, termed a *fascine choker*, is formed of two stout levers about five feet long, connected near their extremities by a chain or strong cord, which should be long enough to pass once round the fascine, and be drawn tight by means of the levers.

78. The twigs are laid on the horse, with their large and small ends alternating; the choker is applied to bring them together; and they are bound by *withes*, or *gads*, made of tough twigs, properly prepared by untwisting the fibres over a blaze, so as to render them pliant; or else stout rope yarn may be substituted for them. The gads are placed twelve inches apart, and every third or fourth one should be made with an end about three or four feet long, having a loop at the extremity to receive a picket through it; this picket is termed an *anchoring picket*, its object being to secure the fascine firmly to the parapet.

79. To form the revetment, the first row of fascines (Fig. 23) is imbedded about half its thickness below the tread of the banquette, and is secured oy means of the anchoring pickets, and also by several pickets driven through the fascine itself about twelve inches into the earth. The knots of the withes are laid inside, and the earth of the parapet is well packed behind the fascine. A second row is laid on the first, so as to give the requisite interior slope; it should break joints with the first row, and be connected with it by several pickets driven through them both. The other rows are laid with similar precautions; and the parapet is usually finished at top by a course of sods.

80. *Hurdle revetment.* This revetment is made by driving poles (Fig. 24), in the same direction as the interior slope, into the banquette, about eighteen inches below the tread, and then forming a wicker-work, by interlacing twigs between them in a similar manner to basket work.

The poles should be nine inches apart, their diameter about one-and-a-half inches. They should be secured to the parapet by long withes and anchoring pickets. The top twigs should be bound together by withes.

81. *Gabion revetment.* The *gabion* (Fig. 25) is a round basket of a cylindrical form, open at each end, its height is usually two feet nine inches, and diameter two feet.

82. To form a gabion, a *directing circle* is made of two hoops, the difference between their radii being such, that, when placed concentrically, there shall be about one-and-three-quarter inches between them. They are kept in this position by placing small blocks of wood between them, to which they are tied with packthread. The directing circle is laid on the ground, and seven or nine pickets, about one inch in diameter and three feet long, are driven into the ground between the hoops, at equal distances apart; the directing circle is then slipped up midway from the bottom, and confined in that position. Twigs half an inch in diameter, and as long as they can be procured, are wattled between the pickets, like ordinary basket work; when finished within about one-and-a-half inches of the top, the gabion is placed with the other end up, the directing circle is taken off, and the gabion is completed within the same distance from the other extremities of the pickets. The wicker work at the two ends is secured by several withes, and the ends of the pickets being brought to a point, the gabion is ready for use.

83. The gabion revetment is seldom used except for the trenches in the attack of permanent works, where it is desirable to place troops speedily under cover from the enemy's case shot and musketry. When used for field works (Fig. 26), a fascine is first laid partly imbedded below the tread of the banquette; the gabion, which is placed on end, rests on this, so as to give it the requisite slope; it is filled with earth, and the parapet is raised behind it, and another fascine is laid on top, and in some cases two.

84. *Plank revetment.* This revetment may be made by driving pieces of four-inch scantling about three feet apart, two feet below the tread of the banquette, giving them the same slope as the interior slope. Behind these pieces, boards are nailed to sustain the earth.

85. *Sand bags* are sometimes used for revetments when other materials cannot be procured; though their object, in most cases, is generally to form a

speedy cover for a body of men. They are usually made of coarse canvass; the bag. when empty, is two feet eight inches long, and one foot two inches wide; they are three-fourths filled with earth, and the top is loosely tied. From their perishable nature, they are only used for a temporary purpose, as when troops are disembarked on an enemy's coast.

86. *Scarp revetment.* This revetment (Fig. 27) is formed of a framework of heavy timber, and is used only for important field forts. A piece, termed a *cap*, or *cap-still*, is imbedded in a trench made along the line of the berm; other pieces, termed *land-ties*, are placed in trenches perpendicular to the cap, with which they are connected by a dove-tail joint; they are about eight or ten feet asunder Cross pieces are halved into the land-ties about two feet from their extremities, and two square piles, about five feet long, are driven in the angles between the land-ties and cross pieces; inclined pieces, which serve as supports to the cap, are mortised into its under side at the same points as the land-ties. These supports usually receive a slope of ten perpendicular to one base; they generally rest on a *ground-sill* at the bottom of the ditch, to which they are mortised; this sill being held firm by square piles. The ground-sill may be omitted, by driving the supports below the bottom of the ditch.

Behind this framework, thick plank, or heavy scantling, is placed side by side, having the same slope as the supports; or else a rabate may be made in the cap and ground-sills, and the scantling be let in between these two pieces serving as a support to the cap. This is the more difficult construction, but it is the better, since, should the heavy supports be cut away, the cap will still be retained in its place.

4*

87. Scarp revetments are sometimes formed by laying heavy timber in a horizontal position; but this method is bad, as it enables the enemy to gain a foot-hold by thrusting their bayonets between the joints.

88. The length of the land-ties should be at least equal to two-thirds the depth of the ditch.

89. The counterscarp is seldom reveted. A framework similar to that for the scarp might be used, and thick boards, laid horizontally, be substituted for the inclined scantling.

90. When a scarp revetment is made, the excavation of the ditch must be conducted in a different manner from that already explained. In this case, after the cap-sill and land-ties are laid, the excavation is continued to the bottom of the ditch, by removing only earth enough to allow the framework to be put up. A scaffolding of plank is then raised in the ditch on which the earth, that remains to be excavated, is thrown, and from there on the berm.

CHAPTER VII.

100. THE means employed as accessory usually consist of artificial obstacles, so arranged as to detain the enemy in a position where he will be greatly cut up by the fire of the work.

101. Anything may be regarded as an obstacle to the enemy by which his attention is diverted from the assailed to his own situation; but no obstacle will be of much service to the assailed which is not within good striking distance of his weapons. The proper disposition, therefore, of obstacles, is in advance of the ditch within short musket range.

102. Marshes, water courses, wet ditches, precipices, &c., may be regarded as obstacles, if they are sufficient in themselves to stop the enemy's progress. But, however strong, they are not solely to be relied on; as the strongest natural position may be carried if not vigilantly guarded.

103. In placing the ground around a work in a defensive attitude, every means should be taken to reduce to the smallest possible number the points by which the enemy may approach; so that, by accumulating the troops on the weak points, a more vigorous defence may be made. In making this arrangement, equal care should be given to everything that, affording a shelter to the enemy, would enable him to approach the work unexposed to its fires. To prevent this, all hollow-roads, or dry ditches, which are not enfiladed by the principal works, should be filled up, or else be watched by a detachment, covered by an advanced work. All

trees, underwood, hedges, enclosures, and houses, within cannon range, should be cut down and levelled, and no stumps be allowed higher than two feet. Trees beyond cannon range should not be felled; or if felled, they should be burnt, to prevent the enemy's movements being concealed.

104. If there are approaches, such as permanent bridges, fords, and roads, which may be equally serviceable to the assailed and to the enemy, they should be guarded with peculiar care; and be exposed to the enfilading fire of a work especially erected for their defence.

105. The principal artificial obstacles are *trous-de-loup*, or *military pits*; *abattis*; *palisades*; *fraises*; *stoccades*; *chevaux-de-frise*; *small pickets*; *entanglements*; *crows-feet*; *inundations*; and *mines*.

106. *Trous-de-loup*. (Fig. 28.) These are pits in the form of an inverted truncated cone, or quadrilateral pyramid; their diameter at top is six feet, their depth six feet, and width at bottom eighteen inches. A stake is, in some cases, planted firmly in the bottom, its top being sharpened, and the point a few inches below the upper circle.

107. Trous-de-loup are generally placed in three rows, in quincunx order, a few yards in front of the ditch. They are readily laid out by means of an equilateral triangle, formed of cords, the sides of the triangle being eighteen feet; the angular points mark the centres of the pits. The earth taken from them is spread over the ground between them, and is formed into hillocks to render the passage between as difficult as possible. If brush wood, or light hurdles, can be procured, the pits may be made narrower, and covered with the hurdles, over which a layer of earth is spread.

Trous-de-loup are sometimes p.aced in the ditch, in this case their upper circles touch.

108. This obstacle is principally serviceable against cavalry.

109. *Abattis.* (Fig. 21.) The large limbs of trees are selected for an abattis. The smaller branches are chopped off, and the ends, pointed and interlaced with some care, are presented towards the enemy. The large end of the limb is secured to the ground by a *crotchet-picket,* and may be partly imbedded to prevent its being readily torn up.

One of the best methods of forming an abattis, and which is peculiarly adapted to strengthen the skirts of a wood occupied by light troops, is to fell the trees so that their branches will interlace, cutting the trunk in such a way that the tree will hang to the stump by a portion uncut. The stumps may be left high enough to cover a man in the act of firing.

110. Abattis are placed in front of the ditch; in this position they must be covered from the enemy's fire by a small glacis. They are sometimes placed in the ditch against the counterscarp.

111. This is an excellent obstacle in a wooded country, and admits of a good defence, if a slight parapet is thrown up behind it. The parapet may be made of the trunks of trees laid on each other with a shallow ditch, or trench, behind them; the earth from which is thrown against the trunks. In an open position it may be relied on as a security against a surprise, particularly of cavalry.

112. *Palisades.* (Fig. 23.) A palisade is a stake about ten feet long, and of a triangular form, each side of the triangle being eight inches. The trunks of straight trees should be selected for palisades. The diameter of the trunk should be from

sixteen to twenty inches. The trunk is sawed into lengths of ten-and-a-half feet, and is split up into rails, each length furnishing from five to seven rails. The palisade is pointed at top, the other extremity may be charred if the wood is seasoned, otherwise the charring will be of no service. A *palisading* is a row of palisades set in the ground, either vertically, or slightly inclined towards the enemy. To plant the palisades, a trench is dug three feet deep; they are then placed about three inches asunder, with an edge towards the enemy. Each palisade is nailed to a strip of thick plank, termed a *riband*, placed horizontally about one foot below the ground; another riband is placed eighteen inches below the top. The earth is firmly packed in the trench.

113. A palisading is sometimes used as a primary means of defence, particularly for low works. A banquette is thrown up for this purpose against it; the tread of the banquette being six feet below the top of the palisading, and four feet three inches below the upper riband.

114. As an obstacle, it is best placed at the foot of the counterscarp; the points being twelve inches below its crest, or else covered by a small glacis. In this position the palisading fulfils all the conditions of an efficient obstacle; it is under the fire of the work; covered from the enemy's fire; will not afford a shelter to the enemy; and cannot be cut down without great difficulty.

115. *Fraise* (Fig. 24.) This obstacle is formed of palisades, placed, in juxtaposition, either horizontally, or slightly inclined. The best position for a fraise is on the berm, or a little below it, so as to be covered by the counterscarp crest. The part of the fraise under the parapet is termed the *tail*, and is about five feet long. To make a fraise, a hori-

a mtal piece of four-inch scantling, termed a *cush-ion*, is first laid parallel to the berm; each palisade is nailed to this, and a thick riband is nailed on top of the fraise near the end.

116. The point of the fraise should be at least seven feet above the bottom of the ditch, and should not project beyond the foot of the scarp, so as not to shelter the enemy from logs, stones, &c., rolled from the parapet into the ditch.

117. *Stoccade.* Trunks of small trees from nine to twelve inches in diameter, and twelve feet long, are selected to form a stoccade. They are planted in juxtaposition, in a similar manner to a palisading, and are used for the same purposes. The manner of arranging a stoccade, which is also sometimes termed a *picket*, as a primary defence, will be described in another chapter.

118. *Chevaux-de-frise.* A cheval-de-frise (Fig. 29) consists of a horizontal piece of scantling of a square, or hexagonal form, termed the *body*, about nine feet long, which is perforated by holes two inches in diameter, and five inches apart; round staffs, ten feet long, and two inches in diameter, termed *lances*, shod with iron points, and inserted into the body, so as to project equally from it. At one end of the body a ring and chain are attached; at the other a hook and chain; for the purpose of attaching several together, forming a chevaux-de-frise.

119. The square is the best form for the body, it requires only five-inch scantling, whereas the hexagon will require twelve-inch timber.

120. The chevaux-de-frise is not much in use as an obstacle, owing to the difficulty of making it. It is a good defence against cavalry; and on rock may supply the place of palisades; but even here

an abattis would be more effective, and generally more readily formed.

121. *Small pickets.* This obstacle (Fig. 26) consists of straight branches of tough wood cut into lengths of two-and-a-half, or three feet. They are driven into the ground, in a quincunx order, about twelve inches apart, and project irregularly above it, not more than eighteen inches. Interlaced with cords, grape-vines, brambles, prickly shrubs, &c., they form an excellent *entanglement.*

122. The *crows-foot* is formed of four points of iron, each spike about two-and-a-half inches long, and so arranged, that when thrown on the ground one of the points will be upwards. They are a good obstacle against cavalry, but are seldom used. Boards, with sharp nails driven through them, may supply the place of crows-feet. The boards are imbedded in the ground, with the sharp points projecting a little above it.

123. *Inundations.* This obstacle is formed by damming back a shallow water-course, so as to make it overflow its valley. To be effective, an inundation should be six feet deep. When this depth cannot be procured, trous-de-loup, or else short ditches, placed in a quincunx order, are dug, and the whole is covered with a sheet of water, which, at the ditches, must be at least six feet in depth.

124. The *dams* used to form an inundation are made of good binding earth. They cannot, in general, be raised higher than ten feet; they need not be thicker than five feet at top, unless they are exposed to a fire of artillery, in which case they should be regulated in the same way as a parapet. The slope of the dam down-stream should be the natural slope of the earth; but up-stream the slope should have a base twice that of the natural slope.

Sluices are made in the dams, in a similar manner to the sluices of a mill-dam, for the purpose of regulating the level of the water in the pool above, in case of heavy rains. *Waste-wiers* are also serviceable for the same purpose, but unless carefully made they may endanger the safety of the dam.

125. The distance of the dams apart will depend on the slope of the stream. The level of each pool should be at least eighteen inches below the top of the dam, and the depth of water below each dam should be at least six feet. These data will suffice to determine the centre line, or *axis* of each dam.

126. Artificial inundations seldom admit of being turned to an effective use, owing to the difficulties in forming them, and the ease with which they can be drained by the enemy. But when it is practicable to procure only a shallow sheet of water, it should not be neglected, as it will cause some apprehension to the enemy. In some cases, by damming back a brook, the water may be raised to a level sufficient to be conducted into the ditches of the work, and render some parts unassailable. The ditches in such cases should be made very wide, and to hold about a depth of six feet. During freezing weather the ice should be broken in the middle of the ditch, and a channel of twelve feet at least be kept open, if practicable. The ice taken out should be piled up irregularly on each side of the channel; and, as a farther precaution against a surprise, water should be thrown on the parapet to freeze.

127. *Mines.* Attempts at applying mines to the defence of field works have seldom proved successful, owing to the rapid character of the assault, from which the mines are usually sprung too soon

5

or too late; so that the only effect that can be counted upon for their use is the panic they may create.

128. There is one species of mine denominated a *stone-fougasse*, which it is thought might be successfully applied to the defence of the ditches and salients of field works. To make this mine (Fig. 30), an inclined funnel-shaped excavation is made, to the depth of five or six feet, at the bottom of the funnel a box containing fifty-five pounds of powder is placed, with which a *powder-hose* communicates. A strong shield of wood, formed of battens well nailed together, is placed in front of the box; and three or four cubic yards of pebbles, or an equal weight of brick bats, or other materials, are filled in against the shield. Earth is then well rammed around the shield on top and behind, to prevent the explosion from taking place in the wrong direction. A fougasse of this size, when sprung, will scatter the pebbles over a surface sixty yards in length, and seventy yards in breadth.

CHAPTER VIII.

INTERIOR ARRANGEMENTS.

129. UNDER the head of interior arrangements is comprised all the means resorted to within the work to procure an efficient defence; to preserve the troops and the *materiel* from the destructive effects of the enemy's fire; and to prevent a surprise.

130. The class of constructions required for the above purposes, are *batteries; powder-magazines; traverses; shelters; enclosures for gorges*, and *outlets; interior safety-redoubt*, or *keep;* and *bridges of communication.*

131. All arrangements made for the defence, with musketry and artillery, belong to what is termed the *armament.*

132. The armament with musketry is complete when the banquette and the interior and superior slopes are properly arranged, to enable the soldier to deliver his fire with effect; and to mount on the parapet to meet the enemy with the bayonet. For this last purpose stout pickets may be driven into the interior slope, about midway from the bottom, and three feet apart. The armament with artillery is, in like manner, complete, when suitable means are taken to allow the guns to fire over the parapet, or through openings made in it; and when all the required accessories are provided for the service of the guns.

133. The armament with artillery is a subject of great importance, because it is not equally adapted to all classes of works. Experience has demon-

strated that the most efficient way of employing
artillery, is in protecting the collateral salients by a
well directed flank and cross fire, which shall not
leave untouched a single foot of ground within its
range, over which the enemy must approach. It
has moreover shown, that a work with a weak profile affords but little security to artillery within it;
for artillery cannot defend itself, and such a work
can be too easily carried by assault to offer any
hope of keeping the enemy at a distance long
enough to allow tne artillery to produce its full
effect.

134. The best position for artillery is on the
flanks and salients of a work; because from these
points the salients are best protected, and the approaches best swept; and the guns should be collected at these points in batteries of several pieces;
for experience has likewise shown, that it is only by
opening a heavy, well-sustained fire on the enemy's
columns, that an efficient check can be given to them.
If only a few files are taken off, or the shot passes
over the men, it rather inspires the enemy with confidence in his safety, and with contempt for the defences.

135. *Batteries.* Tne term battery is usually applied to a collection ot several guns; it is also used
in speaking c the arrangements made of a parapet
to enable the guns to fire over it, or through openings
in it; as a *barbette battery,* an *embrasure battery,* &c.
Two kinds of batteries are used in the defence of
intrenchments, the barbette battery and the embrasure battery.

136. The barbette is a construction by means of
which a piece can fire over a parapet. It consists
of a mound of earth, thrown up against the interior
slope; the upper surface of which is level, and two

feet nine inches below the interior crest for guns of small calibre, and four feet for heavy guns. If the barbette is raised behind a face, its length should be sufficient to allow sixteen-and-a-half to eighteen feet along the interior crest for each gun; and its *depth*, or the perpendicular distance from the foot of the interior slope to the rear, should be twenty-four feet, for the service of the guns. The earth of the barbette at the rear and sides receives the natural slope. To ascend the barbette, a construction, termed a *ramp*, is made; this is an inclined plane of earth, which connects the top of the barbette with the terre-plein. The ramp is ten feet wide at top, and its slope is six base to one perpendicular. The earth at the sides receives the natural slope. The ramp should be at some convenient point in the rear, and take up as little room as possible.

137. As barbettes are usually placed in the salients, an arrangement is made for the guns to fire in the direction of the capital. The construction in this case is somewhat different from the preceding. A pan-coupé of eleven feet (Fig. 31) is first made; from the foot of the interior slope at the pan-coupé, a distance of twenty-four feet is set off along the capital; at the extremity of this line a perpendicular is drawn to the capital; and five feet are set off on this perpendicular on each side of the capital; from these points, on the perpendicular, a line is drawn perpendicular to each face respectively; the hexagonal figure, thus laid out, is the surface of the barbette for one gun. The ramp in this case is made along the capital.

138. If three or more guns are placed in the salient, a pan-coupé is formed as in the last case; and twenty-four feet (Fig. 32) are in like manner set off on the capital; but instead of proceeding as in

5*

the last case, a perpendicular is drawn from this point to each face, and the pentagonal space, thus enclosed, will be taken for the gun in the salient: from the perpendiculars last set off, as many times sixteen-and-a-half feet will be set off, on the interior crest of each face, as there are guns required: this will give the length of the barbette along each face; the depth will be made twenty-four feet, and the two will be united in the salient. One or more ramps may be made as most convenient.

139. The advantages of the barbette consist in the commanding position given to the guns, and in a very wide field of fire; on these accounts the salients are the best positions for them. Their defects are, that they expose the guns and men to the enemy's artillery and sharpshooters.

Light guns, particularly howitzers, are the best for arming barbettes; because the hollow projectile of the latter is very formidable, both to the enemy's columns and to his cavalry; and when his batteries are opened against the salients, the light pieces can be readily withdrawn.

140. The embrasure (Fig. 33) is an opening made in the parapet for a gun to fire through. The bottom of the embrasure, termed the *sole*, is two feet nine inches, or four feet above the ground, on which the wheels of the carriage rest, according to the size of the gun; it slopes outwards to allow the gun to be fired under an inclination, the base of this slope should never be less than six times the altitude; the interior opening, termed the *mouth*, is from eighteen inches to two feet wide, according to the calibre of the gun, and is of a rectangular form; the embrasure widens towards the exterior, which widening is termed the *splay*; the manner in which the splay is regulated, is by producing the

sole to the exterior slope of the parapet, and making this exterior line, measured on the sole, equal to half the distance between the inner and outer lines of the sole. This construction makes the sole a trapezoidal figure; the side of the trapezoid, on the interior being eighteen inches, or two feet; the opposite side being equal to half the perpendicular distance between the two sides. The line which bisects the sole is termed the *directrix* of the embrasure; the sides of the embrasure, termed the *cheeks*, are laid out, by setting off two points on the exterior crest of the parapet, one on the right, the other on the left of the sole, so that the horizontal distance of these points from the sole shall be equal to one-third their height above it. Lines are then drawn, on the exterior slope, from these points to the exterior points of the sole; lines are in like manner drawn from the same points, on the superior slope, to the upper points of the mouth, on the interior crest. These four lines form the boundaries of the two cheeks on the superior and exterior slopes.

141. When the directrix is perpendicular to the direction of the parapet, the embrasure is termed *direct*; when the directrix makes an acute angle with it, the embrasure is termed *oblique*.

142. The manner of laying out an oblique embrasure is similar to the direct; the mouth is of a rectangular form, but is made wider in proportion to the obliquity, in order that the part of the embrasure, which corresponds to the muzzle of the gun, may be nearly of the same width in both the direct and oblique embrasures. The exterior width of the sole is made equal to one half the length of the directrix, measured on the sole. The cheeks are laid out as in the last case.

143. The muzzle of a gun should enter at least six inches into the embrasure, to prevent the blast from injuring the cheeks; this limits the obliquity of the directrix to about 60° for long guns.

144. The height of the cheeks must not be more than four feet, for the same reason; it will, therefore, in some cases, be necessary to raise the ground on which the wheels rest.

145. The parapet of a battery is usually termed the *epaulment*. The interior face of the epaulment, and the cheeks of the embrasures, are riveted in the usual manner. That part of the interior face which lies below the chase of the gun is termed the *genouillère*. The mass of earth between two embrasures is termed a *merlon*.

146. The embrasures are generally cut out after the epaulment is thrown up. If their position is decided upon beforehand, they may be roughly formed at first, and be finished after the epaulment is made.

147. The advantages of embrasures are, that the men and guns are less exposed than in a barbette battery. Their principal defects are, that they have a very limited field of fire; they weaken the parapet; and present openings through which the enemy may penetrate in an assault. Owing to their limited field of fire, they are chiefly used for the protection of particular points; as to flank a ditch. protect a salient, enfilade a road, &c. The most suitable position for them in a work is on the flanks.

148. *Platforms.* When a gun is fired often in the same direction, the ground under the wheels is soon worn into ruts; it is to prevent this, that platforms of timber are used in such cases.

149. The shape of the platform is usually a rectangle; in some cases, where a wide field of fire is to be obtained, the form is a trapezoid. The ectangular platform (Fig. 33) is ten feet wide, and seventeen feet long, for siege pieces; and nine feet wide and fifteen long, for field guns. It consists of three *sleepers* of six-inch scantling, either fifteen or seventeen feet long, which are laid perpendicular to the direction of the epaulment, and are covered with two-inch plank, twelve inches wide, and cut into lengths of nine or ten feet. Between the ends of the sleepers, and the foot of the genouillère, a piece of eight-inch scantling, nine feet long, termed a *heurter*, is laid; it should project about six inches above the platform, and be bisected by the directrix. The object of the heurter is to prevent the wheels from being run against the revetment, and also to give the gun its proper direction, particularly in night firing.

150. To lay a platform, the earth on which it is to rest should be well rammed and levelled; three trenches are then made for the sleepers, two of which should be placed under the wheels, and the middle one under the trail. The sleepers are laid flush with the ground, and firmly secured by pickets driven at their sides and ends, and the earth is solidly packed in the trench around them; the plank is then laid and secured by nails, or some other fastenings.

151. If the platform is for direct firing, with full charges, the *tail* may be made six inches higher than the front to break the recoil; in all other cases it should be horizontal.

152. A platform may be constructed simply of three pieces of timber (Fig. 31), one under each wheel, and one under the trail, firmly secured by pickets, and connected by cross pieces, into which they are halved.

152. For barbettes, the platform may be dispensed with; or, if used, the whole surface nearly of the barbette should be covered.

153. If the platform is made of a trapezoidal form, it will require five sleepers.

154. *Powder magazines.* The main objects to be attended to in a powder magazine are, to place it in the position least exposed to the enemy's fire; to make it shot proof; and to secure the powder from moisture.

155. If there are traverses, such, for example, as are used in defilement, the magazines may be made in them; or they may be placed at the foot of a barbette; or, in dry soils, be made partly under ground.

156. The magazine should be at least six feet high, and about the same width within; its length will depend on the quantity of ammunition. It may be constructed of fascines, gabions, or *coffer work*, or any means found at hand may be used which will effect the end in view.

157. If fascines are used, the sides (Fig. 34) should slope outwards to resist the pressure of the earth; the fascines should be firmly secured by pickets, and anchoring withes. The top may be formed by a row of joists, of six-inch scantling, placed about two-and-a-half feet apart; these should be covered by two layers of fascines laid side by side, and the whole be covered in by at least three feet thickness of earth. The bottom should be covered by a flooring of joists and boards; a shallow ditch being left under the flooring, with a pitch towards the door of the magazine, to allow any water that might leak through to be taken out. A thatch of straw might be used on the inside, but it is somewhat dangerous, owing to its combustibility; hides

or tarpaulins are better, and will keep out the moisture more effectually.

158. A *coffer-work* is formed by making frames (Fig. 35) of six-inch scantling; each frame is composed of two uprights, termed *stanchions*, and a cap and ground-sill, well nailed together; it is six feet wide, and six feet high in the clear. These frames are placed upright, and parallel to each other, about two-and-a-half feet apart; they are covered on the top and sides by one-and-a-half-inch plank which is termed a *sheeting*. The magazine otherwise is constructed as in the last case.

159. When gabions are used, a hole is usually dug in the ground to form a part of the magazine; the gabions (Fig. 36) are placed in two rows, side by side, around the hole, and are filled with earth. The top is formed as in the case of fascines.

160. The mouth of the magazine is covered by a *splinter proof shelter*. This is constructed (Fig. 37) by taking scantling eight by ten inches, cut into suitable lengths, and placing it in an inclined position, so as to cover the mouth, and leave an easy access to it. The pieces, usually, are inclined 45°, and are placed side by side; they are covered by at least two feet of earth, or sods; and hides or tarpaulins are thrown over the whole.

161. Splinter proof blinds are mainly intended to afford a shelter against the fragments of hollow projectiles that explode in the work. They may be used as a kind of barrack for the troops; and to store provisions, &c.

162. *Traverses.* Those which are constructed to cover the flanks of the guns from an enfilade fire, are usually what are termed *gabionades*. To form a gabionade, gabions are placed in a row (Fig. 38), side by side, enclosing a rectangular space of

about twelve feet in width from out to out, and abou. twenty-four feet in length, perpendicularly to the epaulment. A second row is placed within this and touching it. The area thus enclosed is filled in with earth, to a level with the top of the gabions. Four rows of large fascines are next laid on the gabions, to support a second tier consisting of one row. The second tier is filled in like the first, and the earth is heaped up on top, making the gabionade nearly eight feet high. The work will be expedited by throwing up the greater part of the earth before placing the second tier. Splinter proof traverses may be made by placing three thicknesses of gabions side by side filled with earth, with a second tier of two thicknesses on top.

163. *Enclosures for gorges and outlets.* A stoccade is the best enclosure for the gorge of a work. The outline (Fig. 39), or plan of the gorge, should be a small bastion front, for the purpose of obtaining a flank defence.

164. The trunks for the stoccade (Fig. 40) should be ten or twelve inches in diameter, and eleven feet in length. It will be best to square them on two sides, so that they may have about four inches of surface in contact. The top of the stoccade should be at least eight feet above the ground. To arrange it for defence, a banquette is thrown up against it on the interior; the height of the banquette one foot nine inches. A strip, about two feet in length, should be cut from the top of two adjacent trunks, with a saw, so that when they are placed side by side there shall be an opening at top, between them, eight inches wide on the interior, and two and a half inches on the exterior; this opening, through which the muzzle of the musket is run out, in firing, is termed a *loop-hole.* The distance between the

loop-holes should be three feet. In this arrangement the bottom of the loop-holes will be six feet above the ground, on the exterior, to prevent the enemy from closing on them to stop them up, or use them in the attack.

165. About four feet in front of the stoccade, a ditch is made twelve feet wide and three feet deep. The earth from the ditch is thrown up against the stoccade, in a slope, to the level of the bottom of the loop-hole, to prevent the enemy from attempting to cut down the stoccade.

166. *Outlets* are passages made through a parapet, or an enclosure of a gorge, for the service of the work. They should in all cases be made in the least exposed part of the work. Their width need not be more than six and a half feet, when used only for the service of the work; but when they serve as a common passage for wagons, &c , in the case of the intrenchment crossing a road, they should be at least ten feet wide.

When cut through a parapet, the sides receive a slope of three perpendicular to one base, and are riveted with sods, &c.

167. A gate, termed a *barrier*, serves as an enclosure to the outlet. The framework of the barrier is made like an ordinary gate (Fig. 41), consisting of two uprights, or *stiles*, a cross-piece, or *rail*, at top and bottom, and a *swinging bar*, or a *diagonal brace*. Upright palisades, about seven feet long and four inches thick, are spiked to the frame about four inches apart; they are finished at top with spikes. A barrier, thus constructed, will not offer a shelter to the enemy should he attempt to cut it away. The barrier is hung on hinges like an ordinary gate. The posts of the framework should be very solidly braced to support the weight of the barrier.

A cheval-de-frise is sometimes used for a barrier it presents but a trifling obstacle.

168. The outlet should be covered by a mask, thrown up either on the interior, or on the exterior, to prevent the enemy from firing through it into the work. A traverse (Fig. 42) is thrown across it, if placed on the interior. Sufficient space should be left between the traverse and the parapet for the passage of a gun. The length of the traverse is arranged to prevent the enemy from firing into the work, by an oblique fire through the outlet. The traverse may be of earth or of wood; in either case it should be arranged for defence to enfilade the outlet. In some cases, and it would generally be safest, a barrier is erected between the parapet and the traverse, on each side of the outlet.

169. In very frequented passages, a redan (Figs. 48, 49, &c.) or a lunette, is thrown up on the exterior to cover the outlet, and ensure its safety in case of surprise.

170. *Safety Redoubt.* In enclosed works a place of retreat, into which the troops may retire in safety after a vigorous defence of the main work, will remove the fears of the garrison for the consequences of a successful attack of the enemy, and will inspire them with confidence to hold out to the last moment.

171. This interior work, which may very properly be termed the *keep*, can only be applied to works of large interior capacity. It may be formed of earth, or consist simply of a space enclosed by a defensive stoccade, or palisading. In either case it should be about four feet higher than the main work, to prevent the enemy from obtaining a plunging fire in it from the parapet of the main work.

172. The best arrangement for the keep is the

construction termed the *block-house*. This work (Fig. 43) is made of heavy timber, either squared on two sides or four; the pieces which form the sides of the block-house are either laid horizontally, and halved together at the ends, like an ordinary log-house, or else they are placed vertically, side by side, and connected at top by a cap-sill. The sides are arranged with loop-hole defences; and the top is formed by laying heavy logs, side by side, of the same thickness as those used for the sides, and covering them with earth to the depth of three feet.

173. With regard to the details of the construction, the timber for the sides should be twelve inches thick, to resist an attack of musketry, and to resist field-pieces two feet, in which case the sides are formed of two thicknesses of twelve-inch timber. If the timber is placed upright, each piece should be let into a mortise in the cap-sill; and every fourth piece of the top, at least, should be notched on the cap-sill, to prevent the sides from spreading out.

174. The plan of the block-house must conform to its object generally; it may be square or rectangular. (Fig. 44.) If flank defences are required, its plan may be that of a cross. The interior height should not be less than nine feet, to allow ample room for loading the musket; this height will require that the timber of the sides shall be twelve feet long, in order to be firmly set in the earth. Sometimes a ground sill is placed under the uprights, but this is seldom necessary. The width may be only twelve feet in some cases, but it is better to allow twenty feet; this will admit of a camp bed of boards on each side, six-and-a-half feet wide, and a free space of seven feet. If cannon is

to be used for the defence, the width must be at least twenty-four feet; this will allow eighteen feet for the service of the gun, which is generally ample, and six feet for a defence of musketry on the opposite side. A greater width than twenty-four feet cannot well be allowed, because the bearing would be too great between the sides for twelve-inch timber; and even for a width of sixteen feet it would be well to support the top pieces, by placing a *girder* under them resting on *shores*.

175. The loop-holes are three feet apart; their interior dimensions are twelve inches in height, and eight inches in width for sides twelve inches thick; and twelve inches square for sides two feet thick. The width on the exterior, for the same thicknesses, will be two-and-a-half and four inches. The height of the loop-hole on the exterior will depend on the points to be defended; it should admit of the musket being fired under an elevation and a depression. The height of the loop-hole above the exterior ground is six feet.

176. Vents for the escape of the smoke are made over each loop-hole, between the cap-sill and the top pieces.

177. The camp bed serves also as a banquette; it is placed four feet three inches below the loop-hole, and has a slight slope of about eight inches inwards.

178. The provisions, accoutrements, &c., are placed on shelves and racks attached to the shores and girders.

179. The block-house is surrounded by a ditch, similar to the one used for a defensive stoccade. A strong door is made in one of the re-entering angles, and a slight bridge leads from it across the ditch.

180. It has been proposed to place a slight parapet of earth on top of the block-house. It is thought that this accumulation of earth would be too heavy for the timbers, independently of leaving but little space for the defence. Perhaps a better arrangement might be made on top, similar to a defensive stoccade, the uprights being secured at bottom, between two pieces resting on the top pieces, and held firm by an arrangement of riband pieces and braces.

181. It has also been proposed to place the interior and exterior rows of uprights three feet apart, and to fill in between them with closely packed earth, for a defence against artillery. This method has been tried, and was found to be less solid than the one here laid down, independently of being more difficult to construct.

182. The top pieces should in no case project more than twelve inches beyond the sides to admit of logs, &c., being rolled over on the enemy.

183. The block-house is sometimes arranged with two stories, the corners or the sides of the upper story projecting over the sides of the lower. Either of these methods is sufficient for the defence of the lower story; but the first is the best to procure a fire in the direction of its angles. It can only be used, however, as a defence against infantry.

184. When artillery cannot be brought to bear against the top of the block-house, it may be constructed like an ordinary floor, and be covered with nine or twelve inches of earth to guard against fire.

185. The application of wood to the purposes of defence is one of paramount importance in our country. A block-house, surrounded by a defensive stoccade, is impregnable to the attack of infantry

6*

If properly defended, and is therefore peculiarly suitable to either wooded or mountainous positions, where a train of artillery cannot be taken without great labor, owing to the impediments that may be thrown in its way, by rendering the roads impassable from obstructions easily obtained. In positions covered by extensive earthen works, such as those that would be required for the defence of the towns on our sea-board, and which would be occupied during a war, a defensive arrangement of the barracks for the troops, so that they might serve, in case of the main works being forced, as rallying points, under cover of which the main body of troops may retreat with safety, is a subject that commends itself to the serious attention of the engineer. From the details already entered into, an efficient combination for this purpose will suggest itself to the reader, without entering farther into particulars.

186. *Ditch defences.* The surest defence for a ditch is a good flanking arrangement of the work itself; but as this is, in many cases, impracticable, owing either to the relief, or to the plan, flank defences must be procured by a construction made in the ditch. Several methods may be resorted to for this purpose, termed *caponnières, scarp* and *counterscarp galleries.*

187. The caponnière is a work made across the ditch, and may be either single or double. A single caponnière is nothing more than a defensive stoccade, or palisading, made at the extremity of a ditch, as in the case of a redan. It will obviously be of no service, unless the enemy is forced to attack it in front.

188. A double caponnière (Fig. 45) is arranged to fire in two directions, and is usually placed at the middle of the ditch which it is to protect. It is

made in all respects like a block-house with upright sides; its width may be only eight feet, and its height the same.

189. The bottom of the caponnière may be on the same level as the ditch, or below it; in the latter case, the loopholes should not be more than eighteen inches above the level of the ditch, to prevent the enemy from using them against the assailed within. In the former, a small ditch should be made round the caponnière, and the earth from the ditch be thrown against its sides.

190. The plan of the caponnière (Fig. 46) should be arranged to admit of being flanked by a defensive stoccade, placed at the foot of the scarp; for this purpose the end next to the counterscarp should be in the form of a salient flanked by the stoccade. To prevent the enemy from jumping on the caponnière, from the crest of the counterscarp, a space of at least twelve feet should be left between the two. Moreover, the top of the caponnière should be covered from the enemy's artillery, either by the counterscarp crest, or by a glacis.

191. The communication to the caponnière, from the work, may be by a timber gallery under the parapet, formed of frames and a sheeting, similar to the construction used for a powder magazine.

192. The counterscarp gallery (Fig. 47) consists of a framework, covered on top with a sheeting, which is placed within the counterscarp at the salients. The front of the gallery is made of nine or ten-inch scantling, placed upright, and arranged with loophole defences; these pieces are connected at top by a cap-sill. Cross-pieces are notched on the cap-sill, about three feet apart; they are supported by shores placed four feet from the front piece. The cross-pieces may project three feet be-

yond the shores, and, if necessary, be braced from the shores. The gallery is covered on top by one-and-a-half-inch sheeting; and behind in a similar manner, but only to the height of five feet above the bottom. This arrangement gives a free space behind the back sheeting for the play of the rammer in loading. The height of gallery may be only seven feet; its width, according to the foregoing arrangements, is four feet. It should be covered on top by at least three feet of earth. The level of the gallery should be the same as the ditch; and there should be a small ditch in front of it, to prevent the enemy from closing on the loopholes, or obstructing their fire by filling the ditch in front of them by means of sand bags, fascines, &c. The entrance to the gallery is by a narrow door.

A scarp gallery, either for musketry, or for one or two pieces of cannon, may be constructed to procure a flank fire in ditches with dead angles. These galleries may be made in all respects like a double caponnière; the bottom of the gallery being sunk low enough to allow the greater portion of the ditch to be swept. As the top of the gallery must support that portion of the parapet of the work above, it must be firmly shored by strong timber. The rear of the gallery must be open, and there should also be an escape for smoke at the berm of the parapet above the gallery.

A construction of a like character may be used to form a blind for one or two guns which it may be particularly desirable to place under cover from an enemy's artillery. The sides of the blind may be farther secured by placing against them either gabions or sand bags.

CHAPTER IX.

193. DISPOSITIONS made to cover extended positions, and which present a front but in one direction to the enemy, are termed *Lines*. There are two classes of lines—*Continued Lines*, and *Lines with Intervals*. Continued lines present no openings through which the enemy can penetrate except the ordinary outlets. Lines with intervals consist of detached works, which are enclosed partly, or entirely, throughout their perimeters, arranged in defensive relations with each other; and presenting wide intervals between them defended only by their fire.

194. The same general principles apply to lines as to other intrenchments; but, from their great extent, they usually receive a slight relief, and the simplest angular figures are adopted for their plan. In laying them out, the engineer should avail himself of all the natural obstacles presented by the position, so as to diminish the labor of erecting artificial ones.

195. *Continued Lines.* The simplest arrangement for a continued line, consists in a series of redans (Fig. 48) connected by straight curtains; it is termed the *redan line*. The faces of the redans are sixty yards in length; their salient angles 60°; and the distance between their capitals one hundred and eighty yards.

196. This combination will place the salients at one hundred and sixty yards from the collateral re-enterings. An inspection of this system shows that the ditches are not flanked; tnaf the salients are not well protected, owing to the cross fire leaving a considerable sector without fire in front of them; that the curtains, which, from their position, are the strongest points, are the best defended, and in turn they afford no protection to the faces. All these defects become more sensible as the redans are placed farther apart.

197. To remedy the defects of the redan line, it has been proposed to break the curtains forward (Fig. 49) so as to form two branches, one perpendicular to the face of each redan. This suggestion has led to the *tenaille line*, which consists of a combination of small and large redans, or simply of redans of the same size, forming salient and re-entering angles. This combination is superior to the redan line. The salients are protected by a cross fire, and the ditches of the large redans are partially flanked; moreover, it presents fewer assailable points, on a given front, than the redan line; and its retired parts afford good positions for artillery.

198. The faces of the large redans should not exceed one hundred and sixty yards; and their salient angle should not be less than 60°. The faces of the small redans should not be greater than forty yards, and should be perpendicular to those of the large redans. These combinations will give two limits for the length of the capitals of the large redans, and for their distance apart. When the salient angles are 60° the length of the capitals will be about one hundred and thirty-eight yards, and the distance between them two hundred and twenty-eight yards. When the salient angle of the small redan is 60°, the capitals of the large redans will be eighty yards long, and the distance between them three hundred and sixteen yards. In the first case

there will be a greater number of assailable points on a given front, but the re-enterings will be the stronger; in the second case the reverse of this will happen. Of course the size of the redans will not be restricted to the limits here laid down. This system is defective, in presenting very long faces to an enfilade fire, and in taking up a considerable depth of ground, from the salients to the re-enterings, which restricts its application to particular localities.

199. The *indented line* (Fig. 50) is principally used in place of a straight curtain between two advanced works, which are too far apart to protect each other and the space between them.

200. When the ground between the advanced works is level, or nearly so, the branches of the crémaillère form salient and re-entering angles, which are on the same right lines. The long branches alternate from the middle point, where either a salient or re-entering angle is formed; the latter is preferable, as it is strongest, and may be arranged with flanks and a curtain, which will be better situated for defence than the two faces forming a salient angle. When there is a valley between the two advanced works (Fig. 51), the branches of the crémaillère should conform to the slopes of the ground; the long branches should be thrown back, so that their prolongation shall fall within the salients of the advanced works, to avoid an enfilading view of the enemy. The middle point may be arranged as in the preceding case.

201. The crémaillère line is more easily adapted to irregular sites, particularly to the sides of hills, or similar slopes, than either of the preceding dispositions, because it requires but a slight depth of ground.

202. Owing to the imperfect flanking arrangements of the preceding systems, it has been proposed to use bastion lines. They are laid out by placing the salients two hundred and fifty yards apart, and making the perpendicular of the front equal to one sixth.

203. Another arrangement of the bastion line is the one termed *with double flanks*. (Fig. 52.) The salients, in this case, should be between four hundred and five hundred yards apart. The figure explains itself. By this arrangement there are fewer assailable points on the same front; one of the bastions is placed in a strong re-entering; and the salients of the advanced bastions are protected by the flank fire of the collateral advanced bastion, and also of the retired bastion.

204. The principal objection to the bastion line is its great development, and the consequent increase of labor and time for its construction.

205. Continued lines are not suited to an active defence; and this is a grave objection to their use. The enemy, if repulsed by their fire, can retreat in good order, and renew the assault at a more opportune moment; because the assailed, if they attempt a sortie, must defile through narrow outlets, and present a feeble front to the enemy during the operation of defiling. They are, however, an admirable defence for irregular troops, owing to the confidence which they inspire. They also serve to guard against a surprise, and to prevent the predatory excursions of small detachments of the enemy.

206. *Lines with intervals.* The detached works used for these lines may be either lunettes or square redoubts (Fig. 53); their salients are two hundred and fifty yards apart, and their salient angles may usually be 90°. The faces about sixty yards, and

the flanks about forty yards, are so arranged as to sweep the ground in front of the salients of the collateral works. In the rear of the first line, and opposite to the intervals, redans are placed to flank the faces of the first line; the faces of the redans may be about thirty yards. About two hundred yards in the rear of the first line, and opposite the lunettes, cavalry epaulments are thrown up, to cover squadrons of cavalry to act on the flanks of the enemy, when his columns are shaken by the fire of the works.

207. The works of the first line are large enough to contain from three hundred to four hundred men, with a field battery in each, for their defence. The redans are good positions for batteries to flank the first line. Redoubts present an advantage over lunettes, because they are equally strong throughout, but this is accompanied by the defect that their rear faces may be used against the assailed if the enemy should carry them. The gorges of the lunettes should be enclosed by an abattis, palisading, &c., which will not afford a shelter to the enemy should he get possession of them.

208. A system of defence has been proposed by General *Rogniat,* former *Chief* of the *French Engineer Corps,* in his work *Considérations sur l'art de la Guerre,* the spirit of the arrangement of which partakes both of the bastion line with double flanks, and of the line with intervals.

209. Points two hundred and fifty yards apart are taken for the salients of the lunettes; their faces and flanks are placed in defensive relations; and between them a redan, with a pan-coupé, is placed to flank the faces, without intercepting the fire of the flanks; a straight curtain is carried from

7

the redan, and leaves an interva. of ten yards between it and the flanks of the lunettes for sorties.

210. With regard to the profiles, the lunettes receive the minimum profile both for the parapet and ditch. The redans are simple epaulments to cover cannon fired in barbette; and the curtains consist of a trench with the earth thrown in front to form a parapet, which is so arranged that the infantry may march from the trench in order of battle over it.

211. The advantages claimed for this system are, first, the short time required to form the works, by which an army may entrench its field of battle in one night; second, the lunettes form the first line of the order of battle, and contain only infantry, and the batteries are placed in the redans, where they are more secure, protect the lunettes, and withdraw the fire of the enemy's artillery from the lunettes; third, the curtains are defended by infantry, who can sally from them at a moment's warning, and aided by the light artillery and cavalry, who débouche through the intervals between the curtains and lunettes, and attack the enemy in flank. If the flanks of his position are not secured by natural obstacles, Gen. Rogniat proposes to throw up a strong square redoubt on each flank, and to place a heavy battery in the interval between the redoubt and the adjacent lunette.

212. Lines with intervals are peculiarly adapted to well disciplined and active troops. The works thrown in advance constitute the first line of the order of battle, against which the first shock of the enemy is partially thrown away, and he dare not attempt to neglect them, for an endeavor to penetrate through the intervals would expose his flanks to a close and deadly cross fire. If the enemy is repulsed, the main body of the army, which is drawn

up in rear of the works, immediately assumes the offensive, and, by a vigorous advance movement, charges the enemy in turn, relying on the works to cover its retreat if driven back.

213. In every combination of this nature the flanks are the weak points; they should rest, if practicable, on some unassailable point, as a marsh, river, &c.; otherwise very strong works should be thrown up for their protection.

214. It has been proposed, by some writers, to throw up several lines of detached works for the defence of a position; so that the troops in the first line may retreat under cover of the second, and so on. This arrangement, in the first place, can seldom be made, without *weakening the order of battle*, and therefore weakening the defence, by too great a dissemination of the troops. Moreover, in works of great extent there never can be that concert, which is so essential to a vigorous defence, from the impracticability to direct it properly. The troops, destined to act offensively against the enemy if repulsed, are too far in the rear to be brought up in time; and the ground being greatly cut up, by such a multiplication of works, will render the manœuvres slow and difficult. Besides, *a very capital objection in war*, the time and labor required to throw up so many works are altogether beyond what can be disposed of in the ordinary circumstances of an army.

CHAPTER X.

215. THE object of this chapter is to lay down
some general rules respecting the manner of combining artificial and natural obstacles, so as to draw
the greatest resources from both in strengthening a
position.

216. *Mountainous sites.* The crests, and gorges,
are the most important military features of a mountainous position. It is through the latter that the
roads are made, and the former, from their elevation,
command the latter. The crests should therefore
never be abandoned to the enemy, although from
their position, or distance, they may not directly
overlook the gorges; for, independently of the real
advantage of position, which the enemy would thus
acquire, he would possess a relative advantage in
the moral effect produced on troops when they find
themselves in a commanded position.

217. If the base of the mountain does not stretch
out too far from the summit to admit of a sure retreat on the latter, works may be thrown up for the
defence of the base, with intermediate works between the base and the summit placed on the
secondary ridges, or other commanding points.
But if the distance between the summit and
base is great, and particularly, if it is decided beforehand to retreat upon the summits, in case of
disaster, then the base should be disregarded.

218. The works thrown up for the defence of the
summit should be laid out on the brow of the height,

77

for the purpose of overlooking and guarding its sides. In planning the works, the re-entering parts of the brow should be arranged to obtain a cross and flank fire on the slopes in front of the salient points; and particular regard should be had to the inclination of the slopes, in arranging the relief and the means of defence.

219. Very steep slopes will not admit of a defence with artillery, because the gun cannot be fired under a greater depression than one-sixth, and unless the shot take effect the enemy will be inspirited to advance, confiding in the safety of his position. In slopes of this character the works may consist simply of a parapet (Fig. 55), in the form of a glacis, without any ditch, the earth for the parapet being taken from an interior trench; in some cases a dry stone wall may be substituted for an earthen parapet. An abattis may be formed in front of the parapet within close musket range; and heavy round logs, or large masses of rock, be arranged along the parapet, ready to be rolled over on the enemy should he break through the abattis. Steep escarpments of rock are generally considered inaccessible; but those points should never be left to their own strength. It is always prudent to post a small detachment to frustrate an attempt of the enemy to surprise them.

220. A steep natural slope (Figs. 56, 57) may be readily made inaccessible by cutting away the face of the eminence.

221. It may, in some cases, be indispensably necessary to guard certain points at the base of a mountain, as, for example, where the base is washed by a river, over which there is an important ferry. Under such circumstances the point to be guarded should be protected by a strong work; and a chain

7*

of posts, placed on the most commanding points between the summit and the base, should connect the two. These posts should, when practicable, be placed in defensive relations, and in all cases their fire should sweep all the ground between the two principal points. The interior of the posts most advanced, should be exposed to the fire of those in their rear, in order that the enemy may be driven out, should he succeed in forcing his way into any one. As these posts will require a considerable detachment for their defence, care should be taken not to multiply their number unnecessarily, and never at the expense of the main defence.

222. All communications, leading through the mountains, should be carefully guarded, both at their outlets and at the most suitable intermediate points for defence; otherwise the most respectable positions will be liable to be turned by the enemy. If the communications are not of use to the assailed, they may be barred by a line of abattis, or by an artificial inundation, &c.; and they should be watched by a detachment of light troops, whose retreat on the main works should be secured in case of an attack by superior forces.

223. If the communications are of use to the assailed they should be defended by intrenchments, which should command and enfilade them in the most effectual manner.

224. *Forests.* An abattis is the natural intrenchment of forests. The position of the abattis will depend on circumstances. If light troops are in observation in advance of the forest, they may be covered by a line of abattis, to prevent a surprise, and to enable the corps, if driven back, to retire under cover of the forest. Other lines of abattis may be formed at suitable points in the

forest itself. If the forest is in front of intrenchments, the trees must be felled within cannon range,
and an abattis be formed.

225. *Marshes.* An impassable marsh, or bog,
may serve to render a weak point unassailable, if
the enemy can neither flank nor turn it. Like all
points secured by natural obstacles, it should be
vigilantly guarded to frustrate any attempt to cross
it by surprise.

226. *Rivers.* The works planned for the defence
of a river will depend on the object to be attained,
whether it be simply to prevent the enemy from
crossing, or to give the assailed the means of a secure
communication with the opposite shore.

227. The points most favorable to the passage of
the enemy are fords ; and when the river is not
fordable, the points where an elbow is formed, the
re-entering being towards the enemy. To guard
these weak points, works should be placed in a
suitable position to prevent the enemy from approaching the opposite bank ; and in the case of a
ford, the plan of the works (Fig. 58) should be so
arranged that their fire can be concentrated on the
ford ; and, if the assailed have cavalry, a free space
should be left between the water and the works for
the cavalry to act on ; the object being to charge
the enemy whilst in disorder from crossing the ford.

228. To keep open a free communication with
the opposite shore, it will be necessary to throw up
works there, of sufficient strength to allow the
assailed time to effect a safe retreat, should they be
attacked by superior forces. As these works serve
to cover the bridges in their rear, they are termed
tétes-de-pont, or *bridge-heads.* The best points to
erect a bridge-head are the bends, or elbows of the
river, the re-entering being towards the assailed.

The reasons for selecting these points are, that the bridge-head may be protected by a good flank and cross fire from the opposite shore, which from its shape is most favorable for this purpose; secondly, from the manner in which elbows are formed, the point occupied by the bridge-head will commonly be commanded by the opposite shore, and should the enemy succeed in obtaining possession of the bridge-head, he will have all the disadvantages of a commanded position; thirdly, the elbow is not only unfavorable to the enemy, by preventing him from placing a battery in a position to destroy the bridge, but it also may prevent floating bodies, thrown into the current by the enemy with the same view, either by their shock, or by fire, from coming directly in contact with the bridge, as the chances are, that those bodies will strike one or the other shore before reaching the bend.

229 The plan of a bridge-head should be carefully studied on the ground; and it should, as far as practicable, satisfy the following conditions.

1st. Admit of a defence until all the troops have effected a safe passage.

2d. Cover the bridge from the enemy's artillery; so that the retreat may not be cut off by the destruction of the bridge.

3d. Be suited to the end in view; if, for example, its object is to afford the means to small detachments of making incursions on the opposite shore, a small unimportant work will be all that is required; but if a large corps is to pass, either in retreat, or to act offensively, then the works should be arranged with wide intervals, to allow the troops to débouche in mass, and display readily in order of battle.

4th. The flanks of the works should rest upon the banks, to prevent their being turned; and, when practicable, they should be protected by flanking arrangements from the opposite shore.

5th. A strong interior redoubt should secure the bridge against an attempt on the part of the enemy to obtain possession of it by storming the works.

230. The practicability of obtaining flanking arrangements from the opposite shore will materially affect the plan of the bridge-head. If the breadth of the river is over one hundred yards, not much reliance can be placed on a flanking arrangement for musketry; and if the breadth is from six hundred to eight hundred yards, it will still admit of a very effective flank fire of artillery, but not greatly beyond this. For an unimportant work, therefore, which can be flanked by musketry from the opposite shore, a redan or a lunette will be a very suitable form; and if the work can only be flanked by cannon, a priest-cap (Fig. 59), or a redan, with *crotchets*, or flanks, near the extremities of the faces, and perpendicular to them, arranged for musketry, will be a very suitable form. Neither of these works, however, admits of sufficient strength to cover a very important point, whose loss might compromise the safety of an army, or the success of a campaign. The best arrangement for this purpose is either a *simple* or a *complex crown*.

231. The simple crown (Fig. 60) consists of a central bastion, and two half bastions near the banks. In planning this work, the flanks which protect the central bastion should be longer than the other two, as it is hardly probable that the enemy will attempt an attack on any other point but the salient. The batteries on the opposite shore should sweep the ground immediately in front of the faces, and cross their fire in advance of the salient.

232. The complex crown-work consists of a po-

lygon of three or more sides, on each o which a
bastion front is constructed.

233. If the bridge-head is to cover the manœu
vres of a large army, either advancing or retreating
a strong simple crown (Fig. 60), with a system of
detached lunettes, about six hundred yards in front
of it, presents a very suitable arrangement. The
lunettes may be arranged as in the system of General *Rogniat.* The central bastion of the crown-
work should be armed with a strong battery of heavy
guns to protect the lunettes; and heavy batteries,
on the opposite shore, should sweep the ground between the lunettes and crown-work.

234. If there are islands in the river near the
works, they may be fortified with advantage to flank
them.

235. Besides the arrangements already mentioned,
intervals of from ten to twenty yards should be left
between the shore and the works, for the troops to
defile through; the interior of the work is covered
by a traverse in rear of the interval. A small defensive stoccade should be formed immediately at
the head of each bridge, to enable a company of
picked men to defend it until the bridge can be cast
loose from the shore.

236. An interval of at least one hundred yards
should be left between the bridges, if more than one
is used, and about the same distance should be left
between each bridge and the wings of the work.

237. *Villages.* A village may play a very im
portant part in an action, if suitable arrangements
are made for placing it in a defensive attitude, to
prevent the enemy from carrying it by storm. If
the village is not too far in front of the line of battle, it should be strongly occupied; its rear being
left open to receive succors. But if, by occupying

the village, a very salient, and therefore a very weak point, would be presented to the enemy, then it would be best to demolish it; to prevent the enemy from taking advantage of it, to cover his manœuvres whilst advancing, or from throwing a detachment into it, to cover his retreat if repulsed.

238. To admit of a good defence, the houses of the village should be built of brick or stone, and not be too scattered. The enclosures of the gardens should consist of brick, stone, or mud walls, or a thick-set hedge. Wooden villages do not admit of a good defence, on account of the ease with which they may be burnt; but they should not on this account be abandoned to the enemy; for they offer a shelter, if only a temporary one, to troops, and by checking the enemy only for a short time, may render important service. Villages consisting of log-houses are the most defensible.

239. *Military Posts.* The term *military post* is applied to isolated positions, occupied by small detachments, for the purpose of guarding particular points which are of importance during the operations of a campaign, or for a longer or shorter period. These positions are frequently villages, farm-houses, &c.

240. The officer charged with placing a village in a defensive attitude, should first proceed to a careful examination of its environs, for the purpose of ascertaining what natural obstacles, and what facilities, they present to the approach of the enemy. Very slight accidents of ground may be greatly improved by trenches of trifling depth, with a profile similar to Fig. 55, to place troops speedily under cover. When the surface is undulating it should be particularly examined with this view, the officer taking a position at different points and directing

men to approach him, and occasionally stooping to observe how much they will be masked from a fire at various heights above the surface. The side slope of a ridge from the enemy will be the best position for the trench to obtain speedy cover, provided the ground in advance of it can be well swept from its crest. The next points to be considered are the walls, hedges, &c., of enclosures, which may be turned to a useful account for the defence, or which might serve as a shelter to the enemy. After having finished this examination, he will next proceed to lay out his works; arranging their plan so as to draw every possible advantage from the natural and artificial obstacles at hand, to render certain points inaccessible, and to procure a shelter for his troops, and flanking arrangements by means of the walls, hedges, &c. If there should be danger of an attack before these works can be completed, the roads leading to the village, by which the enemy might approach, should be broken up; and cannon should be placed in the best position to guard the most accessible points. The streets of the village should be barricaded, and the houses and walls, in the vicinity of the barricades, should be placed in a defensive attitude. In taking these preparatory measures against a sudden attack, any means that will afford the troops a cover from the enemy's fire should be resorted to; bales of cotton, or wool, casks set side by side, and filled with earth, piles of timber, &c., have been used with great success under such circumstances. As the various arrangements called for under such circumstances will demand great activity on the part of the garrison, care should be taken to distribute the work among the most conversant with it, placing the men who have any skill in the handling of tools at preparing the woodwa and stone defences, and common laborers at throwing up the earthen works, &c.

241. The works that surround the village should be placed so far from the houses that the troops shall not be incommoded either by the splinters occasioned by the enemy's artillery, or by the flames and smoke, should the houses be set on fire. The communications from all the exterior defences to some central rallying point should be carefully arranged, to avoid confusion in retreat, and check the pursuit of the enemy. The garrison should be made perfectly familiar with them, and with the resources they may afford, in case of need. Shortcuts should be made for this purpose by breaking through garden walls, the party walls of houses, &c., and by the erection of barricades at all suitable points to make a stand.

242. *Hedges.* A thin-set hedge cannot be placed in a good state of defence, and should therefore be destroyed, to prevent its interfering in any manner with the defence. A thick-set hedge (Fig. 61), if over six-and-a-half feet high, should be cut down to this height, and the cuttings be set into the hedge to render it less penetrable; a small ditch is dug in front of the hedge, the earth from which serves to form a banquette and a slight parapet, which are thrown up against the hedge. If the hedge is less than six-and-a-half feet high (Fig. 62), it is cut down to the height of four-and-a-quarter feet; a ditch or trench, about three feet wide at bottom, and two feet deep, is dug behind the hedge, and the earth is thrown up against it, as in the last case. A width of two or three feet should be left between the trench and the earth thrown against the hedge to serve as a banquette.

243. A simple ditch behind a hedge will often

8

serve as a good cover for light troops without any other preparation.

244. *Walls.* If a wall is of brick, or stone masonry, or of mud, and at least six-and-a-half feet high, it may be arranged for defence by cutting loopholes through it, at three feet apart. For walls two feet thick, the interior width of the loopholes should be fifteen inches, the exterior width four inches, and the interior height twelve inches, and the exterior should be arranged to allow the fire to sweep as great a space as practicable. The bottom of the loop-hole is four-and-a-quarter feet above the ground. A small ditch, about three feet in depth, should be dug on the outside of the wall, and the earth thrown against it, to prevent the enemy from closing on the loopholes.

245. If the wall is less than six-and-a-half feet high (Fig. 64), it should be cut down to the height of four-and-a-quarter feet; or else a banquette should be made against it. A trench is dug behind it, as in the case of a hedge of the same height; a ditch of about two feet deep should be dug in front of the wall, to prevent the enemy from reaching the assailed with the bayonet, and to place an obstacle to his climbing over the wall.

246. Walls which are eight feet high (Fig. 65), may be arranged with a double tier of fire; for this purpose a banquette of boards, sustained by *trestles*, or by casks, is made, to enable the assailed to fire over the wall; loop-holes are made near the foot of the wall, and a ditch is dug behind it, to obtain a second tier of fire. In this case no ditch should be made on the outside of the wall, because it might enable the enemy to close on the loopholes.

247. If a long line of wall should require flank-

ing arrangemen's, a timber work, termed a *tambour*, is made on the outside; this work is made like a defensive stoccade, with square or round timber about six or eight inches in thickness; the plan of the tambour is that of a redan with a salient angle of 60°. A hole is made through the wall to communicate with the tambour, and loopholes are made in the wall to flank the faces of the tambour.

248. *Barricades.* Wagons, or carts, sunk in the ground up to their axle-trees, and loaded with stones, or earth, will form a very good barricade. A pile of loose stones will serve the same purpose in some cases; also timber laid in piles, lengthwise and crosswise, with the open spaces filled with stones, or earth, forms an excellent barricade.

249. Barricades should be defended from behind with musketry, and cannon loaded with case shot; a work, like a defensive stoccade, will therefore be the best arrangement for them.

Houses. To place a house in a defensive attitude, the doors and windows of the lowest story should be firmly barricaded, and loopholes be made as in the case of a wall. A tambour should be placed before the doors, both for their protection and to procure flanking arrangements if required. The windows of the upper stories should be partly barricaded, to cover the troops within, and loopholes should be arranged as in the lower stories.

250. The roof, if not fire proof, should be torn down, and the floor of the upper story be covered with earth or dung, moist from the stable, to the depth of about two feet.

251. If it is intended to defend the upper stories, should the enemy succeed in forcing the lower, the stairs should be torn down, and slight ladders be

used in their stead; holes should be made through the floor to fire on the enemy in the lower story, or to throw heavy articles, or boiling water, &c., on him.

252. If there are balconies to the windows of the upper stories, or an upper gallery, they can readily be placed in a defensive state by placing thick boards as a shelter on the outside, and cutting holes through the floor to defend the doors and windows of the lower story.

253. If there are no conveniences of this nature, a temporary structure, termed a *machicoulis gallery* (Fig. 67), may be formed, by placing stout pieces of scantling through holes made in the wall, on a level with the floor; these pieces being confined to the floor on the inside, either by nailing them to it or by tying them with rope to the joists; they should project from three to four feet beyond the wall on the exterior, and vertical pieces of smaller scantling, about four feet long, should be nailed to them, on which boards are nailed to cover the troops from the enemy's fire; these boards should be at least three inches thick. The flooring of the gallery is laid on the horizontal pieces, and holes are made through it to fire on the enemy, or to throw grenades, stones, &c., on him.

254. Any similar arrangement which will shelter a man, in the act of firing from a window on the foot of the wall, or in throwing over stones, &c., will serve the same purpose as a machicoulis gallery. A table might easily be arranged to answer the end in view.

255. In arranging a house for defense, everything should be turned to account. The chimneys may be partly torn down on the interior to obtain bricks to barricade the windows. The flooring boards may

be used for the same purpose, and pillows, blankets, books, &c., be thrust in between the boards nailed on the inside and outside of the windows. By tearing away some of the partitions, and taking up some of the joists of floors, heavy timber may be procured for the machicoulis galleries, for buttresses, for the lower barricades, for shores, &c.

256. The intelligence of the officer will readily suggest to him the uses to which the objects at hand may be applied.

257. *Positions and Intrenched Camps.* There is no talent more essential to an officer than that of seizing at a glance the strong and weak points of a position. This talent, known by the name of the *Military coup d'œil*, can be acquired alone by practice and study; for whatever may be said of natural gifts, no apprehension, however quick it may be, can supply the places of these indispensable requisites in every art, and in no one are they more so than in the *Military Art.*

258. Positions derive their great importance from the influence of fire-arms in the decision of battles; for whatever enables one party to deliver its fire with effect against the other, whilst it, at the same time, remains sheltered in any degree from that of its adversary, places the advantage, all other things being equal, greatly on its side; and it is this advantage which should be principally kept in view in selecting a position.

259. Woods, commanding heights, precipices, and villages, constitute the strong points of a position. They serve as points of support against which the wings of the army rest; or else, by covering parts of the front, they serve as the key points in the defence.

260. A wood, if properly intrenched, covers the

8*

infantry from the attacks of cavalry; conceals its manœuvres, and enables it to deliver its fire without being exposed to that of the enemy.

261. Heights, by giving a commanding view of the surrounding ground, increase both the range and the effects of fire-arms; whilst they, at the same time, serve to screen the troops behind them until they are required to be brought into action. Precipices offer similar advantages to heights, and are moreover unassailable.

262. Villages serve as secure shelters for detachments, which, by their fire, cover the manœuvres of the troops in their rear; and, if properly intrenched, will cause the enemy great loss in his effort to force his way into them.

263. Rivers, marshes, hollows, and ravines, are the most unfavorable features of a position, because they prevent a free circulation from one point to another, and thus impede the manœuvres; and they are exposed to the full fire of the enemy. They may however be of service when they are so placed as to support the wings.

264. The best positions are those which, being in due proportion to the force by which they are occupied, command all the surrounding ground within cannon range, the ground descending in a gentle slope to the front, presenting woods, villages, &c., to support the wings, and cover parts of the front, and admitting of a free circulation from one point to another, with secure communications in their rear in case of retreat. If with these advantages, they present marshes, or other obstacles, which will embarrass the enemy's movements, and force him to advance in column, exposed to the fire and free manœuvres of the assailed, they

will unite everything desirable in a favorable field of battle.

265. Troops should always be encamped in order of battle, to avoid the consequences of a surprise. When a camp is fortified, it is termed an *intrenched camp*. The same rules and general principles apply to the choice of a site for a camp, and the manner of fortifying it, as to other positions. These rules and principles have been so fully developed in the preceding part of this work, that there remains nothing more to be said here which would not be a repetition of what has already been laid down.

CHAPTER XI.

266. *Attack.* The subject of the attack admits of two natural divisions; the first of which comprehends all the preliminary steps taken before the troops are brought into action; the second all the subsequent operations of the troops.

267. An attack is made either by *surprise,* or *openly.* In both cases exact information should be obtained of the approaches to the works; their strength; the number and character of the garrison; and also the character of the commander. This information may be obtained through spies, deserters, prisoners, and others who have access to the works; but implicit faith ought not to be placed in the relations of such persons, as they may be in the interests of the garrison; and in all cases they should be strictly cross-examined and their different representations be carefully compared with each other.

268. The best source of information is an examination, or *reconnaissance,* made by one or more intelligent officers. This reconnaissance should, if possible, be made secretly; but as this will not be practicable if the garrison show even ordinary vigilance, it will be necessary to protect the reconnoitring officer by small detachments, who drive in the outposts of the garrison. The object to be attained by the reconnaissance is an accurate knowledge of the natural features of the ground exterior to the works; the obstacles it presents, and the shelters it affords to troops advancing; the

obstacles in front of the counterscarp and in the ditches; the weak and strong points of the works, and the interior arrangements for the defence. If the work is an isolated post, information should be obtained as to the probability of its being succored in case of an attack; the length of time it must hold or to receive succor; and the means it possesses of holding out.

269. *Attack by surprise.* A surprise is an *unexpected attack,* for which the assailed are not prepared. It is, perhaps, the best method of assailing an undisciplined and careless garrison, for its suddenness will disconcert and cause irremediable confusion.

270. Secresy is the soul of an enterprise of this nature. To ensure it, the garrison, if aware of the presence of the troops, should be deceived and lulled into security by false manœuvres. The troops that form the expedition should be kept in profound ignorance of its object until they are all assembled at the point from which they are to proceed to the attack.

271. The winter season is the most favorable for a surprise, which should be made about two hours before day, as this is the moment when the sentries are generally least vigilant, and the garrison is in profound sleep; and the attempt, if at first successful, will be facilitated by the approach of day, and if unsuccessful, the troops can withdraw with safety under the obscurity of night. Should there be danger, from succors arriving in a short time, the attack should be made soon after midnight, when the garrison is asleep, so that the troops may retire before daylight, after having attained their object.

272. As a general rule, the troops for the attack should consist of a storming party, divided into an

advanced party and its support, and be follow ed by a reserve of picked men. The advance of the storming party will open the way, and be closely followed by the support in the assault of the parapet and a reserve of picked men. There should be two guides, one in front of the storming party, with the detachment of workmen under the command of an engineer officer; the other in the rear, under charge of a guard, to supply the place of the first, if killed. The workmen should be furnished with axes, crow-bars, pick-axes, &c., and several bags of powder, of about thirty pounds each, to be attached to palisad-ings, fraises and barriers, to blow them down, if the alarm should be given whilst they are opening a way through them by other means. All the opera-tions should be carried on with despatch and in silence. Should the sentries challenge, they must be secured or bayoneted.

273. Circumstances alone can determine whether it will be advisable to make false attacks with the true one. They will distract the attention of the garrison, if the alarm is given, from the true attack; and a false attack has sometimes succeeded when the true one has failed. When made, one should be directed against the strongest point of the work: as the strong points are usually guarded with less vigilance than the others; and they should all bo made at some distance from the true attack; and orders be given to the detachments making them to proceed to the point of the true attack, should they succeed in making their way into the work.

If the attack succeeds, immediate measures should be taken to place the works in a state of defence, if the position is to be maintained; or else they should be destroyed, as far as practicable, before retreating from them.

274. *Attack by Open Force.* The general arrangements for an open assault, comprehend the operations to gain possession of the works; the measures for maintaining possession of them, and following up the first advantage; and, finally, the precautions to be observed in the event of a repulse.

275. An open assault may be made either with the bayonet alone, or with the combined action of artillery and the bayonet. The first is the most expeditious method, but it is attended with great destruction of life; it should therefore only be resorted to against works of a weak character, which are feebly guarded; or against isolated posts within reach of speedy succor. When tried it will usually be best to make the attack just before day. If it is made by daylight it will, in most cases, be well to scour the environs with a few squadrons of cavalry, to pick up patroles and stragglers who might give the alarm, and then push forward rapidly the assaulting columns. If the assailed seem prepared, light troops should precede the columns of attack, with orders to display in front of the counterscarp, and open a brisk fire on the assailed, for the purpose of diverting their attention from the columns of attack.

276. In an attack with artillery, the troops are drawn up in a sheltered position, or beyond the range of the guns of the assailed; batteries are then established within about six hundred yards of the works, in the most favorable positions to enfilade the faces, and destroy all visible obstacles. The batteries keep up an incessant fire of ball and hollow projectiles, in order to dismount the cannon, and create confusion among the assailed. When the fire of the works is silenced, the troops are brought forward, and demonstrations are made on several points, to divert the attention of the assailed from the true point of attack, and prevent him from concentrating his strength on that point. Several false attacks should be made at the same moment with the real one, and each of them should be sufficiently formidable, in point of numbers, to enable the troops to profit by any success they may obtain.

277. The number and disposition of the troops making the assault will depend, in so great a degree, on local circumstances, and the arrangements of the assailed, that nothing more can be laid down under this head than some general rules.

278. The attack should be led by a storming party, composed of picked troops, or of volunteers for the occasion; this party is preceded by a detachment of engineer troops, provided with the necessary means to make their way through all obstacles, to enable the storming party to assault with the bayonet. If the detachment is arrested at the crest of the counterscarp, by obstacles which must be destroyed before farther progress can be made, the leading files of the storming party may open a fire on the assailed to divert their fire from the workmen; but this operation should only be resorted to from necessity, as it breaks in on that unity so essential in an operation of this character, and impairs the confidence of the soldier in the bayonet, on which his sole reliance, in such cases, should be placed.

279. The storming party should be provided with light scaling ladders, planks, fascines, strong hurdles, &c., for the purpose of descending into the ditch; to mount the scarp; to cover trous-de-loup, small pickets, &c., &c.

280. Another detachment of engineer troops follows in the rear of the storming party; its duties

consist in rendering the passages, opened by the first detachment, more accessible to the troops, who immediately follow it to sustain the storming party. This second detachment is also charged with the care of placing the work from which the assailed has been driven in a defensive attitude, in order to frustrate his attempt to repossess himself of it. The first detachment should be charged with this duty: for, independently of having handsomely acquitted itself in bearing the brunt of the action, it may be required to precede the storming party in the pursuit of the assailed to his interior works.

281. The troops destined to support and, if necessary, reinforce the storming party, advance in one or two lines, with cavalry, and some pieces of artillery on the wings, to repel sorties. The remainder of the troops follow in order of battle, to improve the first successes, or to cover the retreat of the assaulting columns, if repulsed.

282. The salients are generally the points on which the storming party advances, unless some natural feature of the ground should present greater facilities for advancing on a re-entering, or in front of a face. When the ditch is gained, shelter is sought in a dead angle; and if the work is fraised, or resolutely defended with the bayonet, a breach must be made, either by firing beforehand hollow loaded projectiles into the parapet, or by undermining the scarp with the pick. If the intrenchments consist of detached lunettes, an attack should be made on their gorge at the same moment with the one in front.

283. When the assailed are driven from their main works, the storming party should press hotly on their rear, and endeavor to enter pell-mell with them into their interior works, leaving to the troops

9

which follow them the care of retaining possession of the works gained; but, if the intrenchments are supported by other troops drawn up in order of battle, the storming party should halt in the works until it is reinforced by the troops in its rear.

284. There is no danger to be apprehended, in case of a retreat, after an unsuccessful attack on an isolated work. But in an attack on intrenchments, supported by an army, the retreat of the storming party should be covered by cavalry and artillery, until it can find safety behind the main body of the troops, drawn up in order of battle to protect it, and to receive the assault of the assailed, should he attempt offensive operations.

285. In conducting the attack, preparations should be made beforehand for removing all the artificial obstacles that the assailed may have placed before their works, to impede the progress of the storming party. This duty is usually intrusted to the detachment of engineer troops, who are provided with axes, picks, and other suitable tools for this purpose. When the obstacles are of a nature to be easily destroyed by artillery, it should always be resorted to. Abattis, palisades, fraises, and entanglements, when exposed, may be readily torn to pieces by opening an enfilading ricochet fire on them. When cannon cannot be brought to bear on these obstacles, an abattis may sometimes be set fire to, and palisades, &c., be blown in by attaching bags of powder to them. Trous-de-loup may be passed, either by covering them with plank or strong hurdles, or else by directing the men to pass cautiously between them in extended order; small pickets may be broken down, or else fascines may be spread over them so as to form a tolerably

stable road-way; fascines may also be used to cover the points of spikes.

286. The passage of the ditch, and the assault of the parapet, are the most difficult operations. If the ditch is not more than six feet deep, it can be leapt into without danger, and the men can mount the scarp readily with a very little assistance from each other. When the width is not greater than twelve feet, the ditch may be crossed by laying thick plank, or small scantling, over it. When the depth is over six feet, the storming party is usually provided, either with small scaling ladders, or with fascines, sand-bags, or other means, to fill the ditch partly up; or if these means cannot be procured, the detachment dig away the counterscarp into steps, throwing the earth into the ditch, and thus, in a short time, form an easy entrance to it. Wet ditches may be filled up either with sand-bags alone, or more expeditiously by attaching sand-bags to large fascines, or to trusses of hay or straw.

287. The assault of the parapet is made by the aid of scaling ladders, or by effecting a breach, by firing loaded hollow projectiles into the scarp and parapet, which, by their explosion, crumble the earth down, so as to form an accessible ramp; or else the foot of the scarp is undermined with the pick, and the mass of the parapet tumbled into the ditch.

288. *Defence.* The essential point in the defence is to have every part of the works guarded by a sufficient number of troops to resist an attack on all sides. This is of importance not only in isolated works, which can be surrounded, but also in continued lines; for although the enemy will usually make an attempt to enter only at a few

points, st:ll the confusion and delay which might arise from changing the position of the troops, to meet the movements of the enemy, particularly in a night attack, would be extremely hazardous.

289. A vigorous defence will require, at least, two ranks to be drawn up on the banquette throughout the entire extent of the line, with supports, and a reserve proportioned to the importance of the work.

290. The strictest vigilance should be exerted to guard against a surprise; for this purpose sentries should be posted on all of the most commanding points of the works; and on the exterior, at such points as the enemy might approach unseen, as roads, fords, defiles, bridges, &c.; besides these, small detachments of picked men should be stationed to watch these accessible points, and all other places where the enemy might secrete himself, or approach unexposed to the fire of the works. Patroles should be sent out to watch the enemy's movements, and to have an eye on the manner in which the sentries perform their duties. The patroles are particularly charged with the duty of preventing the enemy from reconnoitring the approaches to the works; to do which effectually, without giving unnecessary alarms, they should be ordered to attack with the bayonet alone, unless surprised by an ambuscade.

291. At night the number of sentries should be increased; and redoubled vigilance be used, particularly after midnight. If there are well grounded apprehensions of an attack, *fire-balls* may be thrown out, or fires be lighted in front of the works, to discover the approach of the enemy. Occasional false alarms should be made to keep the garrison on the alert; but this artifice should not be too often prac-

tised, otherwise it might produce a contrary effect besides all useless fatigue should be spared men who are sufficiently harassed by the ordinary duties of their situation.

292. In conducting the defence, each corps should have its particular post assigned to it; and receive special instructions relative to the part it will have to play. Too much attention cannot be bestowed on the part of the commanding officer in seeing that his subordinates are thoroughly conversant with the character of the defences, and of all the resources that can be drawn from their position; and that this knowledge be imparted by them to the non-commissioned officers, and even to the most intelligent among the privates. The fate of a work may depend upon the good or bad conduct of one individual. The reserve is posted in the most convenient position to afford prompt assistance to any point in danger of being forced. The troops drawn up on the banquette should be carefully instructed in their duties; and they should be taught not to look for aid, or relief, from the reserve, until they have repulsed the enemy.

293. If the enemy opens his attack by a warm cannonade, the troops should not be exposed to it, if they can be sheltered near the posts they are to occupy when his columns of attack approach, at which time his cannonade must cease, in order not to injure his own troops. The men should be instructed to reserve their fire until the enemy has arrived at certain points marked out in front of the works, which should not be farther than two hundred yards from the parapet.

294. Sorties, if well timed, will generally decide the fate of the affair. They should be made when

the column is thrown into confusion, or shows any signs of irresolution in its movements; or when its flank, or rear, is carelessly exposed. They are sometimes made to alarm the enemy for his own safety; or to make a diversion in favor of expected succors in blockaded posts.

295. Cavalry is the best arm for a sortie, on account of the rapidity of its movements, and the violence of its shock. When infantry is employed for this purpose, it should use the bayonet alone.

296. Should the enemy succeed in forcing his way into the work, the reserve should attack with the bayonet, before he has time to form; but it must be confessed that success oftener crowns an offensive movement, on the part of the assailed, in endeavoring to regain possession of their works, than any effort to drive back the enemy at the moment, when flushed with success, he has the hope of a certain victory. The only well-grounded prospect that the assailed have of repelling the assault, when the enemy has gained the top of the scarp, is to meet him in an offensive attitude at the point of the bayonet on top of the parapet.

297. The particular arrangements of the defence consist in defending all obstacles, such as abattis, palisadings, &c., by a warm well-aimed fire; as the particular object of these obstacles is to keep the enemy exposed for a longer time to the fire.

298. Large stones, heavy round logs, and loaded hollow projectiles, should be in readiness to be rolled over on the enemy whilst he is in the ditch endeavoring to mount the scarp. Large branches of trees prepared as for an abattis, with chevaux-de-frise, the other obstacles, should be at hand to obstruct the breach.

299. Finally, in an isolated post, if the enemy after having been repulsed, makes a show of block-ading it, or of renewing his attack, and there is no prospect of succor arriving, the garrison should attempt an escape by night.

END OF THE FIELD FORTIFICATION.

CHAPTER XII.

MILITARY COMMUNICATIONS.

300. DESPATCH is of the first importance in all military operations; and nothing contributes more to it than the means of opening practicable and easy communications in every direction.

301. Among the various obstacles by which the free movements of an army may be embarrassed, water courses, marshes and swamps, hold the first rank, owing to the difficulty of finding suitable means at hand to pass them, or of transporting those means in the train of an army.

302. For the passage of water courses, bridges must be constructed; the character of the construction depending on the nature of the river, the particular locality selected for the bridge, and the means at hand.

303. Before adopting definitively the particular locality, the officer charged with the construction should endeavor to gain the most accurate information, on every point, which might in any manner bear upon this selection; for which purpose he will cause a reconnaissance to be made, to determine the breadth and depth of the river, and the character of its bed;—the velocity of the current, the seasons of freshets, with their usual extent and effects;— the character of the banks, their absolute and relative heights, their slope, the approaches to them, the distance between them and the water way, and finally, if they are wooded or otherwise;—the position and size of islands, whether wooded or not; —the extent of fords, their depth of water, and the

nature of their bottom;—the form and dimensions of elbows and indentations;—the artificial obstructions, or dams, &c., the possibility of their being destroyed by the enemy, and the practicability of applying them to the purposes of artificial inundations;—the position, extent, and character of the affluents;—a description of the permanent bridges, and ferries;—whether the river empties itself into the sea, or into another river, the extent and effects of the tide water;—the nature of the permanent and temporary defences along the river;—the kind of boats used in navigating the river, and the time it would require to collect them at a given point;—the proximity of forests to its banks, and the facilities afforded by them for constructing rafts.

304. As a general rule, the elbows, which present their concavity to the side from which the passage is to be made, are the best positions for the bridge, as being most favorable to the defence; but it must be observed that, when the bridge is to remain any length of time, the effects of the current on the banks, at the elbow, should be carefully ascertained; these effects usually consist in washing away the banks on the concave side, and transporting the fragments to the opposite shore, thus deepening the bed on that side, and filling it up on the other.

305. *Military Bridges.* Any structure raised especially for the purpose of affording a passage to troops across a river, may be termed a *military bridge;* but the expression is generally restricted to those temporary expedients for the same end, of whatever character they may be, to which an army is obliged to resort during the active operations of a campaign.

306. The means most frequently resorted to, for

the passage of troops over a river, is a *floating bridge*. This construction consists of boats, rafts, casks, or other buoyant bodies, anchored at suitable distances apart, to serve as points of support to the bridging proper, which is formed of beams, resting on the supports, to which they are firmly connected, as well as with each other, and of a flooring of plank laid across the beams, and fastened to them.

307. Any buoyant body may be used for the supports, but experience is in favor of large flat-bottomed boats, termed *bateaux*, as presenting more advantages than any other. In Europe, bateaux, termed *pontoons*, which consisted of a framework of light wood, covered on the bottom and sides with tin, or copper, were for a long period mostly in use as a part of the bridge train of an army; but they have gradually gone out of use, and the French particularly, whose corps for the construction of military bridges, termed the *pontooneers*, is justly held in the highest estimation, as the most scientific and experienced in Europe, have adopted the bateau of uniform dimensions, with corresponding equipments, for its army boat train.

308. As it is not the object of this chapter to enter fully into the subject of military bridges, which more properly belongs to a separate treatise, it will be confined to describing only such as troops, the least skilled, may construct under the guidance of an intelligent officer.

309. The general properties of all bridges should be strength, stability, and, if they are to be transported on land, lightness.

310. The strength will depend on the nature of the points of support; and on the cross section of the beams, and their *bearing*, or the distance, between their points of support.

The strength should be such as to resist the action of the heaviest loads on the bridge, and also that arising from the current, the waves, and the wind.

311. The essential requisite for the strength of a floating bridge is, that it shall not be loaded with a weight sufficient to injure the timbers or to submerge it. To ascertain the greatest weight that a bridge may be required to bear, the following data may be taken. The average weight of a foot soldier, with his arms, may be assumed at two hundred pounds; and the lineal space occupied by each man, when marching by a flank, eighteen inches; a cavalry soldier, with his horse and equipments, may be taken at fourteen hundred pounds, and he occupies about nine lineal feet in file; a twelve-pounder gun with its carriage, limber, six horses, and three drivers, weighs about eleven thousand six hundred pounds, and occupies about forty lineal feet in march. The weights here given are rather over estimated, so that any error may be on the safe side.

312. The term *bay* is applied to the interval between any two points of supports of a bridge, estimating this distance between the middle points of the supports; for example, in bateau supports, it would be from the centre line of one bateau to the centre line of the other. If we suppose this bay to be forty lineal feet, a very simple calculation will show, that when infantry is marching by a flank, in the ordinary formation of three ranks, there will be about eighty men on the bay, or sixteen thousand pounds in weight; and comparing this with the weight of either artillery or cavalry, it will be found to exceed them both. This may therefore be as-

sumed as the greatest weight that the bridge will have to bear on each bay.

313. By a principle of hydrostatics, the weight of the volume of water displaced by a floating body is equal to the weight of the body itself; if, therefore, the cubic contents of the part of a bateau, which is above the water line after the bridge is finished, be estimated, and this volume be multiplied by sixty-two-and-a-half pounds, the weight of a cubic foot of water, the result will show the weight, which, in addition to that of the bridge, would submerge it; and as the weight, placed on each bay, is borne by the half of each bateau of the bay, it follows, that if a weight, thus obtained, were laid on each bay, it would submerge the entire bridge. Now, in practice, it is found that a bridge cannot bear with safety a weight greater than three-fourths of four-fifths of that which would submerge it. This consequently will furnish a ready means of comparing the weight that would submerge a bridge with what it can safely bear.

314. To secure the stability of the bridge, every precaution should be taken to prevent an oscillating or undulating motion in any direction. These precautions will, moreover, add to the strength of the bridge, as the connection of the parts will be firmer, and the weight consequently more uniformly distributed over the supports.

315. Oscillations in a lateral direction are prevented by anchors placed above and below the bridge, to which the supports are moored. The object of the up-stream anchors is, principally, to resist the action of the current, and of those down-stream to resist that of the winds and waves. The number, in each case, will therefore depend on the

force of the current and on the width of the river and its exposure to high winds.

316. The inclinations of the cables, by which the supports are attached to the anchors, should be the same for all; so that they may offer a uniform resistance to a pitching motion. This inclination is, ordinarily, taken one-tenth; that is, the distance of the anchor, from the support, is ten times the depth of the water. When the width of the river, and the nature of its banks, render it practicable, a cable is stretched across it, by means of a windlass, and the supports are either attached to this cable, by separate fastenings, or else the cables which attach them to the anchors are passed over and fastened to it.

317. Undulations in a longitudinal direction are prevented by connecting the beams firmly to each other, and to the points of support. This connection will also increase the strength, by diffusing the weight thrown on one support over several. The manner of regulating the passage of troops will, in a great degree, contribute in preventing this motion. Infantry should always pass in open order, and with the route step; cavalry should dismount and lead their horses; and artillery, in some cases should be drawn over by men.

318. Lightness is an essential quality in the bridge equipage which is to follow an army, but it should always be subordinate to strength and stability.

319. *Bateau Bridge.* As the bridge equipage of the French is considered the best arranged, a description of the bridge itself will be here given, to convey a more complete idea of this kind of structure.

320. The bateau is thirty-one feet long, two feet
10

six inches deep, five feet four inches wide at top, and four feet wide at bottom. It is built something like a *skiff*, the head and stern being a few inches higher than the body; the width at the head being two feet, and at the stern four feet. The ribs are of oak; the bottom and sides of pine plank one inch thick.

321. The beams, termed *balks*, which are laid abross the bateaux, are of four-and-a-half inch scantling, and twenty-five-and-a-half feet long.

322. The flooring of the bridge is formed of boards, termed *chesses*, cut in lengths of fourteen feet, the width being twelve inches, and thickness one-and-a-half inches.

323. The bateaux, when the bridge is formed, are thirteen feet ten inches apart, making the distance between their centre lines, nineteen feet two inches.

324. Each bay has five balks, the centre lines of the balks being two feet ten inches apart; and the ends of the balks project six inches beyond the outside gunwales of the two bateaux on which they rest.

325. To confine the chesses to the balks, pieces of scantling, termed *side-rails*, are placed on them, over the outside balks, to which they are fastened by a cord, by what is termed a *rack-lashing*.

326. The distance between the side rails is about eleven feet, and is the width of the free road-way. The chesses project equally beyond the outside balks.

327. Before the construction of the bridge is commenced, a road-way of easy access, the slope of which may be only one-sixth, should be cut through the banks if necessary. An *abutment* is then formed by laying a heavy beam in a horizontal position

perpendicular to the direction of the bridge. The length of this beam should be the same as the chesses; it is imbedded in the earth, on the same level as the top of the bridge, and is confined in its place by a stout picket driven at each end of it, and by two others driven in front of it. A chess is laid flat behind the beam, and with it constitutes the abutment.

328. To give the proper alignment to the bridge, a staff is placed at a short distance from the abutment in the direction of the centre of the bridge, with another some yards in the rear of it and on the same line.

329. The bateaux are placed in the water below the point which the bridge is to occupy, and they are brought successively into their proper position, as the bridge is carried forward from the shore. The first bateau is placed, when the depth of water will admit of it, so far from the abutment that the balks resting with one of their extremities on it, the others will project six inches beyond the outside gunwale of the batteau. The positions of the outside balks are shown by *pintles* placed in the gunwales. The chesses are laid on within one foot of the first bateau; the position of the second bateau is then determined, and the balks of the next bay are laid; the precaution being taken to lay all the balks of the second bay either on the up-stream, or the down-stream side of those of the first bay. The chesses of the second bay are then laid, within one foot of the second bateau, and the construction is thus regularly carried on.

330. As the balks are laid they are fastened to each other, and also to the bateaux, by a rack-lashing; iron *crotchets* being placed on the inside of the bateau for this purpose.

331. The bateaux are fastened to each other by two *spring lines*, stretched diagonally from the head of one bateau to the stern of the other, through iron rings placed in suitable positions on the outside of the bateaux. The four bateaux nearest the shore are tied to strong stakes on shore by two ropes for each bateau, one up-stream, the other down. An anchor is allowed up-stream to two bateaux, and one down-stream to four.

332. When a cable, or *sheer line*, can be stretched across the river, before commencing the bridge, the preceding operations will be greatly expedited; each bateau being attached at once to the cable, by ropes termed *head-lashings*.

333. The side rails are laid so soon as the third bay is commenced; they are fastened to the outside balks by a rack-lashing; the chesses being so arranged as to admit its being passed between them. Each rail should be tied at its middle point, and near each of its ends.

334. When the flooring is completed, it is covered either with a thin layer of straw, or sand, to protect it in some degree from wear and tear.

335. The bridge here described underwent a series of rigid experiments to test its properties; the results of which were of the most satisfactory character, as to its strength, stability and lightness.

336. When the bridge was completed the draught of the bateaux was nine-and-a-half inches; when traversed by a column of infantry three abreast, marching with the cadenced step, and in close order, the draught of the bateau was one foot seven inches, and was the same when crossed by a twenty-four-pounder, drawn by eight horses, with their drivers.

337. Its travelling equipage can follow in the

train of an army with the same ease as a twelve-pounder.

338. A bridge across a navigable stream should admit a free passage to the river craft; for this purpose a part of the bridge, resting on one or two bateaux, should be so arranged that it can be slipped out of its place, forming a *draw* for the passage.

339. To break up the bridge, the operations are the reverse of those for laying it. The operation is commenced at the shore to be abandoned; the side rails, chesses, balks, &c., are taken up in their proper order, and conveyed to the opposite shore, either by hand, or in the bateaux.

340. On narrow rivers, with a gentle current, this operation can be greatly expedited by detaching the entire bridge from its moorings, and allowing it to swing round against the shore. To perform this manœuvre with safety, two stout ropes, or *guys*, are attached, one to the stern, the other to the head of the second bateau, from the shore to be abandoned; ten or twelve men are placed at each guy, to ease off, or *belay*, according to circumstances. Another stout rope, attached to the fourth or fifth bateau, from the opposite shore, is drawn tight and fastened to a strong stake up-stream, at fifty or sixty yards from the bridge. When these preparations are made, the head lashings are cast loose; the two extreme bateaux are detached from their abutments; and the anchor cables are gradually eased off, to allow the bridge to swing round with a gentle uniform motion.

341. This manœuvre requires great care, and should not be resorted to, except in cases of necessity, unless the current is gentle, and there are not more than twenty-five or thirty bateaux. The same

means may be taken, under similar circumstances, to throw a bridge across a river.

342. *Boat Bridges.* Flat-bottomed boats are more suitable than keel-boats for a bridge, owing to their greater volume, and their stability in the water; but when they cannot be obtained, keel-boats may be taken. If the gunwales are not suitable to serve as points of support to the balks, a framework should be placed in the centre of the boat for this purpose. The framework may consist of a sill-piece of six or eight-inch scantling, fitted to the bottom of the boat, and a cap-sill of the same dimensions, which is supported at a suitable height by uprights of four-inch scantling mortised into the cap and sill pieces. This frame is kept in place by *struts*, of the same sized scantling as the uprights, which are placed against the uprights and ribs of the boat.

343. The balks are laid on the caps, jutting about two feet beyond them, and are firmly secured to them and to each other by a rack-lashing.

344. As the boats are generally of unequal size, two small boats may be, in some cases, lashed together to form one support; and to bring them all to the same level, they may be ballasted with stone. The strongest boats should be placed at the extremities of the bridge, as these parts are more liable to injury, from the motion of the bridge, than the middle.

345. When anchors cannot be procured, mill-stones, strong baskets, or bags, filled with large round pebbles, or broken stone, may supply their places; and, in shallow rivers, each boat may be fastened to stout stakes driven into the bed of the river.

346. *Raft Bridge.* Rafts formed of solid timber, or of casks, barrels, the skins of animals prepared and inflated, &c., are frequently used in military operations, either to construct bridges, or to serve the place of boats in the transportation of troops across streams.

347. Timber rafts are particularly serviceable in wooded and mountainous countries, where, owing to the nature of the streams, boats cannot always be procured. A bridge may be constructed on rafts over rivers of any size, and may be made to bear any loads; but, owing to the form and dimensions of the rafts, rapid currents present great difficulties to their manœuvre whilst the bridge is under construction.

348. The timber for a raft may be either square or round, seasoned or green; in all cases, however, the lightest and best-seasoned wood should be preferred as being most buoyant.

349. To ascertain the weight which will submerge a piece of timber of given dimensions, the following method may be used: Take a cubical block, of any size, and ascertain its weight; fill a vessel with water, and immersing the block in it, find the weight of the water which it displaces; the difference between the weight of the block and that of the water displaced, will give the weight which, placed on the block, would be sufficient to submerge it. If this difference be multiplied by the weight of a cubic foot of water, and the product be divided by the weight of the water displaced, the quotient will give the weight necessary to submerge a block of a cubic foot; therefore, multiplying this result by the number of cubic feet in the given piece, the product will be the total weight sought.

350. The cubic contents of the piece itself, if it be the trunk of a tree, may be found by adding into one sum the areas of the two ends, and four times the area of the section, at the middle of the trunk, and multiplying this sum by one-sixth the entire length.

351. The weight of green wood is greatest when it is cut whilst the sap is running ; and seasoned wood, when placed in water, is found to augment about one-sixth in weight, in a few days, unless the precaution is taken to tar the ends of the trunks , and this increase of weight is found to be greater in wood that has been long cut than in new timber.

352. The volume of the raft should be in proportion to the weight of load that the bridge must bear ; and the length and breadth, for the same volume, will be determined from the consideration, that the stability varies directly as the length, and inversely as the breadth ; therefore, the longest and largest trunks should be selected, since fewer of them will be required for the same load, and the length will thus be increased at the expense of the breadth. The length of the trunks should not be less than forty or forty-five feet, particularly if the current is rapid, otherwise there will be a very sensible oscillating motion of the bridge.

353. Before constructing the raft (Fig. 69) the trunks are placed in the water, as they will there assume their natural position of stability, and they can be more easily moved about in it. The large ends of the trunks are cut away on their under side, like the shape of a child's whistle. The trunks are then laid side by side with their butt ends together, leaving about four inches between them, and so that they will project a little beyond each

other from the middle to the outside trunks, making an angle, of the perpendicular of which is one-fourth the base. The trunks are then united by four cross-pieces, one placed near each end, and two near the middle, about ten feet apart; the cross-pieces being fastened to the trunks, either by strong wooden pins driven into auger holes made through the pieces, or else by a strong rope-lashing. Three sleepers are laid across the centre cross-pieces, one over the middle of the raft, and the other two near the outside trunks; the object of these sleepers is to give the flooring sufficient elevation above the surface of the water to prevent the waves from breaking over it.

354. The rafts are anchored by two anchors for each, one up-stream, the other down, the cables of which should be drawn tight to prevent any pitching motion. The rafts should be placed as far asunder as practicable, to allow a free passage to the water; this distance will depend chiefly on the size of the timber that can be procured for balks; each balk should jut at least one foot beyond the middle sleepers of the two rafts on which it rests. The balks are secured to the sleepers and to each other by rack-lashings. The rafts should moreover be connected by a beam at the head and stern.

355. The tendency of the current on the up-stream cables is to submerge the head of the raft; this tendency will be in part counteracted by placing the butt ends up-stream, and by the manner of arranging these ends; as a farther precaution, the flooring should be placed lower down-stream than the centre of gravity of the rafts, so that its weight may tend to raise the head of the rafts.

356. On navigable rivers, a draw must be made similar to the one used for a boat bridge; but as

a *raft-draw* would not be easily manœuvred, particularly in a strong current, it would be well to use a draw of boats.

357. Rafts of empty casks, or inflated skins, may be made to bear any load, by lashing a sufficient number together. They cannot be relied on for a safe passage except on narrow and gentle streams.

358. *Flying Bridges.* Any floating body which is propelled from one shore to the other by the force of the current alone, acting obliquely to its side, is termed a *flying-bridge*. But in order that the flying-bridge shall cross and recross always at the same points of the shores, it must be held by a cable, attached to an anchor, either in the middle, or at some more suitable point of the stream.

359. A flying-bridge, when arranged in the best manner, should bear the heaviest loads that the service may require; it should be perfectly stable, and cross the stream in the shortest time possible.

360. The most usual manner of forming a flying-bridge is to connect two boats, by a platform, consisting of joists laid across the boats, and a flooring of plank on the joists. The cable is attached to this platform, and passing over a cross-piece, supported above the platform by two uprights, so as to sweep clear of the deck in the movement of the bridge, is secured at the other end by an anchor, or any other fixed point of support.

361. The best form of boat is one with a long, narrow, flat bottom and sharp head; the length from sixty to ninety feet; width, ten to fifteen feet, and depth, six to seven feet. These boats have great capacity, and present a large side surface to the action of the current.

362. The distance between the centres of the

boats cannot be much greater than twenty-five to thirty feet, owing to the usual dimensions of the beams used for joists, which will not generally admit of a greater bearing. The length and breadth of the platform are about the same, and may be about fifty feet.

363. The bridge may have two platforms, like the double decks of steamboats, and when arranged in this way, by proper management, it may be made to bear from one thousand to fourteen hundred infantry.

364. The time of crossing will depend on the length of the cable, the position of the anchor, and the direction given to the head of the boat, by means of a rudder, whilst in motion.

365. The cable should be at least equal to the width of the river, and experience has shown that the most suitable length for a quick passage is once-and-a-half the width. If the velocity of the current is the same on both shores, the anchor should occupy the middle point of the stream; but if it is greater near one than the other, then it is best to place the anchor nearest to the shore where the velocity is the least, because in approaching that shore the position of the boat will be in favor of the lessened action of the current.

366. Ordinarily one anchor is deemed sufficient; but as the action of the boat will tend to shift the position of its *shank*, and consequently weaken the hold of its *flukes*, it would be better to place three together, the shank of the middle one being in the direction of the current, and those of the other two being respectively in the directions of the extreme positions of the cable.

367. The height of the cross-piece, which supports the cable, will depend on the velocity of the

stream, and the length of the cable; its object being to keep the cable clear of the platform. A height varying between twelve and thirty feet is generally sufficient. The best position of the cross-piece and its supports, is about one-third the length of the boat from the bow. One cross-piece is enough to support the cable; but as the motion of the boat would occasion rapid wear and tear, both of the cable and the cross-piece, a better arrangement consists in placing two cross-pieces, with a sliding pulley, or *block*, between them, the cable passing through an eye in the pulley.

368. A windlass is placed on the platform, towards the stern, to which the cable is fastened; it serves to let the cable out in case of danger, from the action of the current or wind, and to take up the *slack* when necessary.

369. In shallow gentle streams, or in wide rivers, *buoys*, or narrow small decked-skiffs, are used to buoy up the cable, and prevent it from impeding the velocity of the bridge, by dragging on the bottom. They are placed about one hundred and twenty feet apart, their number depending on the circumstances of the case. The cable should be borne on small supports slightly elevated above their decks.

370. Flying-bridges of boats, or rafts, abandoned solely to the action of the current, may be found very serviceable in effecting a passage by surprise; the bridge is cast loose from the shore and directed on the opposite one, by means of an oar astern, to keep it in the proper position to receive the most favorable action of the current. The platform in this case may be surrounded by an enclosure of timber, or bags of wool or cotton, so as to be proof against the enemy's musketry and case-shot in case of an alarm.

371. *Trestle Bridge.* The form of a *trestle* is the same as what is termed a *carpenter's-horse*, that is, a horizontal beam supported by four legs.

372. The horizontal beam, termed the cap or *ridge-beam*, is usually of eight-inch scantling, and from twelve to sixteen feet long. The legs are of four-and-a-half-inch scantling; they have a spread towards the bottom, the distance between them across being equal to half the height, and lengthwise of the cap, their inclination is one-twelfth of the height; they are fastened to the cap, about eighteen inches from the ends, by nails, the side of the cap and the top of the leg being properly prepared for a strong, accurate fit. The legs are connected either in pairs, or else all four by horizontal pieces of three-inch scantling; sometimes diagonal pieces, going from the top of one leg to the bottom of the opposite one, are used.

373. Bridges on trestles are principally useful in crossing small streams not more than six feet deep. They also serve to connect a boat bridge with the shore, in shallow water; and are used as the supports for the bridges of communication across the wet and dry ditches of field works. They present the advantage of being formed of materials which can always be procured at hand, either by cutting down forest trees, or by demolishing the floors and partitions of houses. Moreover, when constructed of light wood, they may be taken to pieces, and be easily transported on horses, or mules, in a wooded or broken country.

374. The trestles should not be placed farther apart than sixteen feet between the ridge beams, for balks of the ordinary dimensions; the balks should jut at least one foot beyond the ridge beams. The

flooring, fastenings, &c., are the same as in a boat bridge.

375. When the bed of the river is of soft mud, or is hard and uneven, it is difficult to place the ridge beams horizontal; in the former case to make the legs sink equally, they may be let into sills, which should jut a few feet beyond them.

376. The action of the current is counteracted, either by anchors, or else by attaching each trestle to two cables, stretched across the stream above and below the bridge; stout stakes, or piles, might also be used for the same purpose. Another plan consists in making an open *wattling*, or a net work, of tough twigs, or cords, around the legs, near the bottom, and filling it in with broken stone.

377. The best manner of placing the trestles in deep water is by means of a raft, or a boat, so prepared that the trestle can be readily lowered into the water over the side.

378. *Temporary bridges* are readily constructed in wooded countries. The officer charged with establishing communications of this character, will always do well to imitate the ordinary constructions of the country, particularly if he has to employ the country people to form them. In swamps and marshy grounds, a road-way of timber or stout brushwood, or even of trusses of hay or straw, will frequently have to be resorted to. After opening a way of sufficient width, and cutting down the stumps, so as not to impede the passage of vehicles on wheels, the trunks of the largest trees are cut into lengths of about fifteen feet, and are laid across the line, at distances of ten or twenty feet apart; notches are cut into the cross-pieces, about eighteen inches from each end, and sufficiently large to receive trunks of trees from nine to twelve inches in

diameter; these trunks should be cut into pieces of as great length as the tree will afford. Across these longitudinal pieces the bodies of small *saplings*, from three to four inches in diameter, and fourteen feet long, are laid, and small brushwood, earth, or straw, may be laid over them, to make the road-way more regular. In some cases the road-way may be formed by laying the saplings without any other substructure.

379. *Fords.* Infantry can ford a stream when the depth of water is not greater than three or four feet; cavalry when the depth is not more than four feet; and artillery, a depth of two-and-a-half feet. In cases of great emergency, particularly in gentle currents, infantry and cavalry may pass fords of greater depths than those just laid down; but safety and a regard to keeping the ammunition in a good state, prescribe the depths here given.

380. The bottom of a ford should be of solid gravel; if of mud, fine sand, or obstructed with large fragments of stones, the difficulty of passing carriages and large bodies of troops will, generally, be found insurmountable.

381. Fords are frequently met with near elbows, and usually in an oblique position to the thread of the stream. In making a reconnaissance for the purpose of seeking for a ford, a small boat should be allowed to float down with the current, and soundings be made.

382. To prevent accidents whilst the troops are crossing, stakes should be placed in the direction of the ford, showing its width; ropes are fastened to these stakes, on a level with the water, to prevent loss of life. If the ford is crossed at night, lighted torches are tied to the stakes.

383. If a large body of troops should cross, the

infantry should pass first, the artillery next, and the cavalry last, so that the bottom may not be cut up by the feet of the horses.

384. *Ice.* The heaviest guns may cross on ice which is six inches thick, and rests on the water under it; but, as a measure of prudence, plank should be laid under the wheels to distribute their pressure over a greater surface, and also to counteract the effect of shocks.

385. When the ice is but three inches thick, infantry and light guns can cross it with safety; but the men should be sent across in small detachments, and plank, or straw, should be placed under the wheels of the guns and the feet of the horses. By sprinkling water over the straw, it will, by its freezing, form a more compact roadway. Heavy guns must be carried over on *sleds*, taking every precaution to distribute the weight of the load over a large surface.

386. Ice which does not rest on water cannot be trusted to, unless it is at least six inches thick, and even then it should be crossed with great caution.

387. An army should never trust either to fords, or to ice, for keeping open its communications; for a freshet, or a thaw, would place it in the most critical state.

388. *Preservation and Destruction of Bridges.* Floating bridges are liable to injury from oscillations, caused by high winds, and the crossing of troops; from sudden freshets; and from the shock of floating bodies.

389. Besides the usual means which are taken to insure strength, by preventing oscillations, the manner of conducting the passage of troops requires great attention. Infantry should pass in half battalions, with an interval of forty or fifty paces

between each half battalion, and in order of route, by a flank. Cavalry should dismount, and lead their horses, leaving forty or fifty paces between each squadron. Carriages should not cross at the same time as troops, and in no case should they be suffered to pass each other; the intervals between them will depend on the weight of each. Finally, the pontooners should be at their posts, to keep the cables and spring-lines well stretched, and to tighten the rack-lashings.

390. A firm anchorage, and a solid construction are the best securities against the action of high winds, and the sudden rise of the river. To prevent the effects of the latter, the pontooners ease off the cables as the river rises; and when danger is apprehended for the safety of the bridge, it must be cast loose, and suffered to swing round to one of the banks, every possible precaution being taken to prevent its gaining a great velocity during the movement.

391. *Pumps* and *scoops* should be provided to bail out in case of leaking or the breaking in of the waves.

392. In shallow streams, a stockade may be formed, either obliquely across the river, or else with an angle up-stream, at four hundred or five hundred yards above the bridge; strong cables, or chains, are attached to the stockade, on a level with the water, to arrest heavy floating bodies, which might injure the bridge by striking against it. In deep water a *boom* must be placed to secure the bridge. The strength and character of the boom will depend upon the probable means the enemy may have for breaking through it. In some cases a heavy chain buoyed at intervals by logs, or a strong cable sustained in a similar way, and fasten-

11*

ed by ropes to anchors, may be requisite. In others
heavy logs firmly secured to each other at their
ends by chains may offer sufficient security. The
ends of the boom must be strongly attached to large
piles driven into the banks.

393. Posts of observation are placed to watch
the stockade, or the boom. They are provided with
boats, ropes with grapnels, and a few pieces of artillery, for the purpose of arresting all floating
bodies.

394. If a flying-bridge is placed in connection
with the boat-bridge, it should always be below it;
so that no accident may occur from the flying-bridge
parting from its cable.

395. To destroy a bridge of the enemy, heavy
floating bodies, *fire-boats*, and *infernal machines*, are
resorted to.

396. When the object is to destroy the bridge by
a shock, a raft is formed of several large trunks of
trees. A short and strong *mast* is strongly attached
near the head of the raft, for the purpose of carrying away the flooring, if the raft should pass between the intervals of the boats. Large boats,
heavily laden with stones, may be used for the
same ends; the object in both cases being to acquire
sufficient momentum to destroy the bridge.

397. Fire-boats loaded with combustible matter,
are sent down with the current to burn the bridge.
Hollow projectiles, heavily charged with powder,
are placed in the fire-boats to deter, by successive
explosions, the pontooners from approaching them.
Infernal machines are arranged so as to explode by
the shock of the boat against the bridge.

In an attempt to destroy a bridge by these means,
a number of them should be sent down at once, to
increase the chances of success. They are con-

ducted by boatmen as near to the bridge as they can approach with safety, and are then abandoned to the action of the current.

398. When a bridge is no longer of service, it may be destroyed, to prevent its being of use to the enemy, either by sinking it, burning it, or blowing it up. Combustible matter and cannon will serve for the two first mentioned methods, and a barrel or two of powder, placed below the flooring, and fired by means of a powder-hose, or a slow-match, will answer for the third.

399. A stone-bridge can be destroyed by making a trench, eighteen inches deep, across the road-way, over the crown of an arch; placing three hundred, or four hundred pounds of powder in it, and covering it over with plank, and a heavy weight of earth, and exploding it by means just mentioned. Or, if pressed for time, several barrels of powder exploded at the same time in the open air, over the crown, will effect the same purpose.

400. *Passage of Rivers.* There is no military operation of a more delicate character, and of more doubtful success, than the passage of a river in the face of the enemy, whether acting offensively, or in retreat.

401. A passage by *main force* must always be accompanied by the most bloody results, if the enemy displays even ordinary courage and good conduct; and it cannot be attempted, with the slightest prospect of success, unless the troops are covered by a very superior artillery, so posted as to cross its fire in advance of the point where the passage is to be effected, to prevent the enemy from charging the troops in the act of disembarking, before they can form in order of battle. The main difficulty in this operation consists in getting the troops,

first landed, to stand firm until, by successive reinforcements, they find themselves in sufficient strength to advance on the enemy. And the best plan to gain this indispensable time, if the ground be favorable, is to throw over some squadrons of cavalry among the first, which, by successive charges, may keep the enemy at a distance.

402. In attempting a passage, by main force, a point must be selected on the opposite shore where the banks are not steep, wooded, or broken, and where the water is sufficiently deep to float the boats to a firm landing, in order that the troops may be able to form readily in order of battle, and to push forward without danger from a surprise.

403. When the opposite shore is occupied by the enemy in force, and is vigilantly guarded, there remains no way to effect a passage but by *stratagem*. To effect this, the bridge equipage is transported, secretly, to some point near that where the passage is to be made. If there are affluents near this point, or islands, they may be taken advantage of to launch the boats undiscovered, and even to construct the bridge in parts which are afterwards floated to their position and put together. Demonstrations are made on several points, by the army, to draw off the enemy's attention from the real point, and troops are thrown over, after night-fall, in row-boats, and on flying-bridges; and the bridge is immediately commenced, and should be in readiness for the passage of the army by early dawn.

404. To protect the operation from a surprise, the troops first thrown over should occupy all the most accessible approaches, within twelve hundred or fifteen hundred paces, in advance of the point of passage; and other troops should throw up a slight intrenchment, like the *parallel* used in a siege,

about two hundred paces in advance of the ground to be occupied by the tête-de-pont. The object of these works is to keep the enemy off, should he present himself in force; and to gain time for all the army to pass over, and form, without confusion, in order of battle under cover of these first dispositions.

405. A retreat across a river is necessarily made in the face of the enemy; and here, more than in any other position, an army is called on to show the coolest and most determined courage, for its safety depends on the strictest observance of good order. After the bridges are ready, and the tête-de-pont is in a defensible state, the movement of retreat commences, under cover of batteries of heavy guns on the opposite shore, these batteries having been thrown up at the earliest opportunity, and placed to take the enemy in flank.

406. The garrison of the tête-de-pont forms the rear guard, and retires last, leaving a few companies of grenadiers in the stoccade works, at the head of each bridge, for the protection of the pontooners, whilst they are preparing the bridge to be swung round.

In a retreat, a single bridge should never alone be relied on, as the slightest accident happening to it might compromise the safety of the whole army.

CHAPTER XIII.

MILITARY RECONNAISSANCES.

407. By the term *Military Reconnaissance*, is understood a detailed examination of any extent of country, whether large or small, with a view of ascertaining its resources for the movements and subsistence of troops. This examination may be of a *special nature*, as, for example, a proposed line of march; the character of a defile, river, or an enemy's position, &c.; or it may have a more general bearing, as the collecting of information for an entire campaign, or the exploring of a large district of country.

408. The importance of accurate reconnaissances, of whatever nature they may be, cannot be too strongly insisted upon; for all military operations must be based upon them, and any oversight, or neglect, in this respect, may involve the safety of an army, and through it the destinies of a nation.

409. When the reconnaissance is of a special character, the officer charged with it should confine his operations strictly within his instructions, and not waste time upon any object which might with propriety be brought into view in a more general reconnaissance; but when the object is to obtain information for the operations of a campaign, or for distant expeditions, nothing should be overlooked which may bear, even in a remote degree, on the movements and subsistence of an army.

410. A reconnaissance consists of two parts: a *map*, and a *descriptive memoir*.

411. The map should exhibit the topographica

features of the country; and the memoir should supply whatever features cannot be shown on a map, and also furnish information on the resources of the country for the subsistence and movements of troops.

412. The style of the memoir should be concise and clear; and nothing should be contained in it which is not strictly relevant to the object in view. The information furnished by it should be, first, those topographical features which a map cannot so well exhibit, as the nature of the face of the country; the quality of the soil; the height and declivities of mountains; on what side they are accessible, and for what kind of troops, and the means of transportion over them; the character of forests, water courses and other obstacles. Second, the lines of communication, as roads, rail-roads, canals, navigable streams, and all the circumstances in connection with the subject of transportation; the advantages and defects of military positions for the offensive or defensive. Third, everything which relates to the culture and produce of the country; its fertility or barrenness; its resources in provisions and forage; the size and population of the cities, towns, villages, &c. Fourth, the commercial and manufacturing resources of the country; the number of mechanics of the different trades that are most necessary for the supplies of troops.

413. Such is an outline of the operations of reconnaissances in general; and from it may be gathered the acquirements which the officer, charged with making them, is supposed to possess. To a familiar acquaintance with the duties of the topographical engineer, he should unite a large fund of general information on statistics and the

natural sciences; a fund which nothing but a use of daily study and observation can supply.

414. The reconnaissances required by the daily operations of a campaign, are usually of a special character; such as examining a line of march or a military position. A special reconnaissance consists, for the most part, of a sketch in pencil, made with all the accuracy that the means at the disposal of the officer admit of; and a memoir.

415. Before commencing the reconnaissance, all the previous information, which can be obtained from maps, and published descriptions of the country, should be carefully collected, and afterwards compared with the officer's operations; this will serve, not only to abridge the labor, but also to give greater or less confidence in the published information on parts which cannot be examined for want of time, or from other causes.

416. In examining the face of the country, *carriers, wood-cutters, hunters, trappers* and *Indians,* are the best persons to apply to for information, and they should be chosen for guides. To obtain information on the resources of the country, *magistrates, clergymen, inn-keepers, tax-gatherers* and *farmers,* should be questioned; but from whatever source the information may be derived, it should be received with due caution, and only be acted on when confirmed by strict cross-examination of all the parties from whom it comes.

417. The nature of a special reconnaissance has already been shown in the two preceding chapters, and but little more need therefore be added under this head; particularly, as special instructions, arranged under a tabular form, should always be supplied to the officer, charged with the operation, both as a guide to himself, and to enable the officer to

whom the report is made to see at a glance the exact state of the case.

418. The reconnaissance of the enemy's position is one of the most important of a special nature. The officer charged with this service should be thoroughly skilled in the duties of *out-posts;* as his operations must, in most cases, be carried on under the protection of a detachment, subject to his orders. In performing this service, he should never lose sight of the sole end in view, *the obtaining of information on a particular point,* and all his dispositions should be made to attain this end. For this purpose he must vigilantly guard against a surprise, and avoid an action with the enemy, unless the safety of himself and his detachment shall render it necessary; for the procuring of the required intelligence, which is to regulate the movements of the entire army, is paramount to every other consideration.

419. In reconnoitring the enemy's position, the extent of the ground which he occupies, and its character, should be first ascertained; the character of the approaches to his position, and the disposable means that can be found at hand to take advantage of the approaches;—the disposition of his troops, and the arrangement of his defences;—the towns, villages, and other unoccupied sites along his line which might be occupied with advantage by either party;—the character of his line of retreat, and the defensible positions in his rear;—the possibility of turning his position, and cutting his line of operations. In conducting this examination, the officer, of course, will be called upon to make other special reconnaissances of a more minute character; on the nature of the roads, by-paths, bridges, defiles, rivers, fords, marshes, swamps, forests, &c.;

in which will be minutely stated the facilities they may severally afford, and the obstacles they present, to the movements of troops of all arms. The form of these minute examinations must be furnished the officer; for no presence of mind, and tenacity of memory, are sufficient to call to mind all that is necessary to be done in an operation which, from its very nature, must be of a hurried character.

420. A reconnaissance of a position to be defended temporarily, or to be occupied as an intrenched camp, is made with the same care as one for offensive operations. It should state, not only the advantages and defects of the position itself, but should point out the character of other positions in its rear, that might be occupied to check the enemy's progress, should he force the first.

421. The *Military Sketch* of a reconnaissance should be made with all the accuracy that the means at the officer's disposal will admit of. Surveying instruments are not always to be found in an army, and their places must be supplied by the officer's own ingenuity; distances are ascertained approximately, either by pacing them off with a uniform step, and estimating them by the length of the pace, or by the time required. The position of objects may be laid down by the intersections of lines, or by estimating in a rough manner the angles between different points. Slopes and declivities may be judged of by the greater or less time which it may take a man, or a horse whose action is well ascertained, to ascend or descend them.

422. A *pocket sextant*, a small *protractor*, and an *ivory scale*, are invaluable instruments for this service. They not only furnish the means of greater accuracy, but they essentially abridge the labor and time required with less complete means.

CHAPTER XIV.

OUTLINES OF THE GENERAL PROPERTIES OF PERMANENT WORKS AND THE METHOD OF ATTACKING THEM.

423. THE term *Permanent Fortification* belongs to that branch of the *Art of Fortification* where means of a durable character are used to strengthen a position. Permanent differs from Temporary Fortification, not only in the character of the means used, but also in offering a more formidable obstacle to the enemy from the greater strength of its profile.

424. This difference occasions a great disparity, both in the measures and the time required for the attack of permanent and field works. In the latter, a hasty assault decides the fate of the affair; in the former, the enemy is obliged to provide vast resources both of men and materials, and to approach the work attacked slowly, and with the greatest caution, under the cover of intrenchments, by which his troops are sheltered from the fire of the work, and he is enabled leisurely to destroy its defences.

425. Permanent works may be divided into two general classes, *Fortresses* and *Forts*. The term fortress is applied to fortified towns alone, and the term fort, to a work containing only a garrison.

426. The character of the fortification is the same in both classes; consisting, in its most simple form, of an elevated and wide mound of earth, termed the *rampart*, which encloses the space fortified, of an ordinary parapet surmounting the rampart, and of a wide and deep ditch which surrounds the whole.

427. These parts of the profile serve the same purposes as the corresponding parts in the profile of a field work; the most striking difference between the two consists in the rampart, which, from its height, gives a very commanding position to the parapet, and greatly increases the obstacle presented to the enemy.

428. To give both strength and durability, the scarp and counterscarp are revetted with walls of masonry which sustain the pressure of the earth, protect it from the effects of the weather, and, by their height and steepness, present an insurmountable obstacle to an assault by storm.

429. A fortification thus constituted would be sufficient for the protection of troops within it; but would not admit of exterior operations, because it affords no shelter beyond the ditch. Therefore, to procure the facility of manœuvring on the exterior, a low work, in the form of a glacis, is thrown up a few yards in front of the ditch, and completely enveloping it. The space between this work and the ditch is termed the *covered-way*, because it is covered from the enemy's view.

430. The simplest form, then, of an effective profile for permanent fortification, consists of a covered-way; a wide and deep ditch, with a scarp and counterscarp of masonry; and a rampart, which, from its height and width, will give a commanding position to the parapet, and sufficient room behind the parapet for the necessary manœuvres of the troops whilst in action.

431. The general principles of permanent fortification, as now practised, are the results of centuries of experience in the attack and defence. The problem presented for the solution of the engineer consists in making such a disposition of his works that no point within the range of their cannon shall affford a shelter to the enemy; that they shal. enclose the greatest space with the smallest perimeter, without sacrificing the reciprocal protection of the parts, afforded by a flanking arrangement within the medium range of arms; that no defensive dispositions, which can be destroyed by the enemy's distant batteries, shall be exposed to their fire; and finally, that the works shall be secure from an attack by storm.

432. To satisfy these conditions, it was found that the space to be occupied must necessarily be enclosed by a series of bastions connected by curtains; that the line of fortification must be continuous, and consist of a wide and deep ditch, and a high and steep scarp of masonry, to be perfectly secure from an escalade; and that the masonry of the scarp, which is the only part that can be destroyed by a distant fire, must be covered from this fire by the glacis of the work which forms the covered-way.

433. From the range of the fire-arms that are used in the defence, it was found that the distance between the salients of the bastions should not exceed four hundred yards; and that for a reciprocal flanking arrangement, the length of the curtains should not be less than twelve times the absolute relief.

434. To secure the work from escalade, experience has fully proved, that the scarp wall should not be less than thirty feet high, and that the top of it should not be above the crest of the glacis.

435. With regard to the dimensions of the rampart, they must depend on those of the ditch, and a suitable regard to that economy by which all human efforts are circumscribed. The width of the rampart required for the free manœuvres of troops has

12*

been fixed at about forty feet; and its height should
give the parapet a command of at least twenty feet
over the exterior ground.

436. The dimensions of the parapet are the same
as those for the profile of field works of the strongest class.

437. The fortification by which the space fortified
is immediately enveloped, is termed the *Body of the
Place*, or the *Enceinte*. It is seldom that a perma
nent work consists simply of an enceinte, with its
ditch and covered-way, particularly if some of its
points are, from their locality, weaker than the rest.
Other works are usually added to strengthen these
weak points; they are termed *Out-Works* when
they are enveloped by the covered-way, and *Detached* or *Advanced-Works* when placed beyond it.

438. The object of these works is to lengthen
the defence, by forcing the enemy to gain possession of them before he is able to make a breach in
the enceinte.

439. The principal out-work is one in the form
of a redan, termed the *Demi-Lune*, which is placed
in front of the curtain. This work adds to the main
defence by a cross fire on the bastion salients, which
are the weak points of the enceinte, and when there
are demi-lunes on adjacent curtains, the bastions
between them are placed in strong re-enterings,
thereby forcing the enemy to gain possession of the
demi-lunes before he can penetrate, without great
labor and loss of life, into these re-enterings. The
main entrances to the work are usually through the
curtains, which being the most retired parts are also
the most secure; the demi-lunes also serve to cover
these entrances, and to guard them from a surprise.
This, at first, was the only use to which the demi-
lune was applied; but engineers soon discovered

.hat, by enlarging it, new properties were developed, which at length caused it to be regarded as an indispensable accessory in the defence of weak points.

440. The demi-lune, when of suitable dimensions, has also several other important properties, upon which it does not come within the scope of this chapter to dwell. Its ditch is sometimes on the same level with the main ditch; sometimes it is higher; but in all cases the communications between the two, and also with the demi-lune itself, are arranged so as to be easy and secure.

441. Situated between the two flanks of the bastions, and directly in front of the curtain, a small low work, termed the *Tenaille*, serves to mask the scarp wall of the curtain and flanks from the enemy's batteries along the crest of the glacis. This mask is of very great importance, since, by preventing the enemy from making a breach in either the flanks or curtain, it will force him to make it in the face of the bastion; the flanks will thus be preserved for the defence of the breach, and the enemy will not be able to turn the temporary, or permanent works, which may be constructed within the bastion to prevent him from gaining possession of the main work, by an assault of the breach, which he would be able to do could he effect a breach at the same time in the curtain or flanks.

442. The covered-ways of the bastion and demi-lune form a strong re-entering at their point of junction, of which advantage is taken to arrange a small redan whose faces flank the glacis of the two covered ways. The space enclosed by this work, which is a part of the covered-way itself, is termed the *Re-e¯ tering Place of Arms*.

443. The parts of the covered-ways in front of

the salients of the bastion and demi-lune, are termed the *Salient Places of Arms.*

444. The places of arms are so called, because they serve for the assemblage of bodies of troops who are to act on the exterior.

445. Small permanent works, termed *Redoubts,* are placed within the demi-lune, and the re-entering place of arms, for the purpose of strengthening those works.

446. It is a received military principle, that the garrison of a work is no longer in safety, when it can be carried by storm, unless they are provided with a secure point of retreat. It is to effect this purpose that redoubts are constructed. The one in the re-entering place of arms secures the covered-ways from an attack by storm; and that in the demi-lune forces the enemy to advance gradually, and with the greatest precaution, to gain possession of the breach in the demi-lune, and being provided with flanks, which, from their position, have a reverse fire on the breach in the bastion face, the enemy is forced to make himself master of it before he can venture to assault the breach in the bastion.

447. Works, termed *Interior Retrenchments,* which have the same properties as a redoubt, are constructed within the bastion. When the interior retrenchment is sufficiently elevated to command the exterior ground, it is termed a *Cavalier.*

448. The protection afforded by a redoubt to another work, is not by offering a place of safety into which the garrison of the work can retire when driven out of it; but in covering the retreat of the garrison by a warm fire, which will check the advance of the enemy, and enable it to retire behind the redoubt, and not into it; for such an operation would inevitably create confusion in the redoubt,

and might jeopard its safety, as the enemy, in a hot pursuit, might enter it pell-mell with the retreating troops.

449. The crest of the glacis is broken into an indented line for the purpose of obtaining a flank and cross fire on the ground in front of the places of arms.

450. Traverses are placed at intervals along the covered-ways; they serve to intercept the projectiles which enfilade the covered-ways, and also to defend them foot by foot; enabling the troops to retreat from one part of the covered-way behind the traverse under the protection of its fire.

451. The communications of the works consis of arched under-ground outlets, termed *Posterns,* of *Ramps,* and *Stone Stairs.* These communications are placed in the most secure parts of the works, so that the ingress and egress may be without danger.

452. With regard to the relief of the outworks, as a general principle those most advanced should be commanded by those most retired. This principle is applied in all the works, except the tenaille and the redoubt of the re-entering place of arms. The former must not mask the fire of the bastion flanks along the main ditch; and the latter must not mask the fire of the bastion faces upon the glacis of the demi-lune covered-way. To satisfy these conditions, the two works must be commanded by the demilune, which is more advanced than either of them; but, by the process of defilement, they are both so arranged that the enemy will not have a plunging fire into them from the demi-lune.

453. All the fortification, comprehended between the capitals of two adjacent bastions and the glacis

is termed a *Front of Fortification*, or simply a *Front*. It is taken as the unit in permanent fortification.

454. The usual method of effectually protecting any point, is by a flank fire; but, owing to the locality, or to some other cause, it may not be practicable to make a flanking arrangement; to supply its place, dispositions, termed *Counterscarp Galleries*, are made behind the counterscarp, with loophole defences for a reverse fire. This arrangement approximates the nearest to the military solution of the problem *to see without being seen*, since from the position of these galleries, the enemy will not be able to bring his batteries to bear on them, whilst they will present a formidable impediment to all of his operations in the ditches.

455. For seacoast defences, embrasures are made through the scarp wall, and the artillery is protected from shells by an arched bomb-proof covering over head. This arrangement is termed a *Defensive Case-mate*. This method of defence is only efficacious against a sea attack; for on the land side, where the enemy can approach regularly, case-mates would be immediately destroyed by his batteries, and the loss of life would be far greater in them than in an open defence, owing to the fragments of stone which each shot striking an embrasure would cause.

456. Case-mates are also used simply as bomb-proof shelters for the troops and materiel; and no small fort indeed which can be bombarded is tenable without them.

457. ATTACK. The measures for the defence resorted to in permanent works, are of a character to resist, with a certainty of success, multiplied attacks, with the most powerful means, if made openly. This certainty forces the enemy to provide

a large number of troops and materiel; and to approach the work slowly, and always under cover making himself master of the exterior ground foot by foot, and proceeding forward only after having made such a disposition of his troops and works in his rear as to repel all the efforts of the garrison to delay his progress. This method is termed the *Attack by Regular Approaches*.

458. A *Siege* is the operation of cutting off al. communication with a work, and attacking by regular approaches. When the enemy confines his operation to a simple interruption of the communications, it is termed a *Blockade*.

459. The operations of a siege may therefore be classed under two heads; those which are necessary to prevent all ingress to, or egress from, the work, and those which are required to gain possession of the work.

460. The first class of operations comprehend the *Investment*, and the establishment of the *Besieging Army* in intrenched camps around the work.

461. The investment is performed by detaching a strong corps in advance of the besieging army, who, by a sudden movement, surround the work, and seize upon all the avenues leading to it. The object of the investment is to cut off all communication with the work, and to secure everything without it that might in any way prove of service to the garrison. To effect this, the enterprise should be conducted with despatch and secresy; and the troops selected for it should be composed principally of cavalry and light troops, depending, however, on the character of the country; the number of troops being in proportion to the strength of the garrison, and the means that they can employ to oppose the investment.

462. During the day-time, the investing corps will keep beyond the range of the cannon of the works, occupying the most favorable points to prevent excursions from them. At night the detachments will close in upon the work, so as to form a continuous chain of sentinels around it. Engineer officers, who accompany the investing corps, will make a complete reconnaissance of the work, and the exterior ground, for the purpose of facilitating the ulterior operations.

463. In the meantime, the besieging army takes up its line of march, and arriving within the vicinity of the work, the different corps are distributed around it in camps, which are selected beforehand, beyond the range of the garrison's cannon. The besieging army immediately proceeds to intrench itself, by throwing up works to prevent succors of troops, provisions, &c., being thrown into the place ; and also other works to restrain the excursions of the garrison.

464. The first line of works, to prevent succors, is termed the *Line of Circumvallation ;* the other is the *Line of Countervallation.* The first is usually a continuous line, as it is most suitable for the end in view ; the second consists of detached works to cover the weak points of the camp, and particularly the parks of the engineers and artillery, in which all the siege train of these two arms are collected. These lines are about six hundred yards apart to leave room for the camps.

465. The camps of the different corps are connected by removing all the obstacles between them, and opening communications for a free circulation of the troops, so that succor can be promptly despatched to any point which is in danger from an attack by a superior force.

466. Whilst the lines are constructing, the engi neer officers are engaged in making a complete survey and plan of the work and its approaches; and in superintending the preparation of all the materials required for the construction of their own works, so that they may be carried on with vigor after they are begun.

467. The object of the survey and plan is to enable the general, superintending the siege, to select the most suitable point to approach the work. This point is termed the *Point,* or *Front of Attack*. In selecting it, regard must be had to the strength of the point itself; the nature of the ground over which it must be approached; and the more or less ease with which the requisite *materiel* can be brought to this point.

468. The salients are usually the weakest points of a work, because they are easily enveloped by the enemy's approaches, and he will therefore be able to concentrate a heavy fire on them. Solid rock, a stony, or a marshy soil, present the greatest difficulties to the construction of the works of attack. And a good road, or navigable stream, affords the greatest facilities for the transportation of all the materiel required during the siege.

469. The object of the besiegers being to gain possession of the point of attack, with the least sacrifice on their own side, the whole of their measures should tend to the attainment of this end. To effect this, the troops must be able to approach the work under shelter; its fire must be silenced; and a breach be made in its rampart.

470. The works under whose shelter the troops approach the work attacked, are named *Trenches* (Fig. 73), of which there are two classes, the *Parallels* and the *Boyaux*. Each class consists of

13

a ditch, or trench, of uniform depth, and a parapet of uniform height, formed of the earth taken from the trench, and thrown up towards the work attacked.

471. The parallel is a long line of trench, concentric with, or parallel to, the works of the point of attack, which it envelopes; and the boyaux are simply communications, in a zigzag direction, which lead to the parallel. The parallels and the boyaux both serve as a covered way, in which the troops can circulate with safety; but the boyaux are used exclusively for this purpose, whereas the parallels serve to contain troops who restrain the excursions of the garrison, and protect the workmen whilst carrying forward the approaches.

472. The fire of the work is silenced, by selecting suitable positions, near the parallels, from which the faces of the work can be enfiladed, and its guns be dismounted by a ricochet fire.

473. The breach can be made when, the approaches having arrived at the crest of the glacis, the scarp walls are exposed to breach batteries, constructed along this crest, which firing through the ditches of the work, batter away the scarp to its very foot.

474. To lay out the trenches the alignement of the faces and capitals of the front of attack, as well as those of the collateral works, whose fire bears on the ground over which the approaches must be carried, are accurately marked out on the ground by stout pickets, and the distances from the most advanced salients to some point on their capitals are also determined.

475. The object of procuring these alignements is to mark the position and direction of the trenches and batteries. The boyaux are run in a zigzag

direction across the capitals; because this is the shortest line to the salients of the work attacked, which are the points first reached; and in this position they are less exposed to the fire of the work, and are less in the way of the other works of the attack, than they would be if run on any other line.

476. The position of the boyaux and parallels is laid out on the ground with pickets, to which cords are attached, or simply with pickets alone. The position of the *First Parallel* is six hundred yards from the most advanced salients; it should embrace within its extent the faces of all the collateral works that protect the point of attack.

477. At the distance of six hundred yards, the fire of the work is not very troublesome; and it is within good range for a ricochet fire, if it be found necessary to erect the enfilading batteries near the first parallel.

478. Boyaux lead from this parallel to points in the rear of it, about fifteen hundred yards from the work attacked. At these points all the implements and materials of the engineers are collected, and they are therefore termed the *Depots of the Trenches.*

479. The approaches are begun by what is termed the *Opening of the Trenches.* The workmen are assembled at the depots, are supplied with intrenching tools, and are marched and stationed along the line of boyaux, and that part of the first parallel which is to be first made. This is done just at the close of day; and troops, drawn up in order of battle, are stationed a short distance in advance of the workmen to protect them from the sorties of the garrison. The word is then passed along the line of workmen who commence opening the trenches,

which, from this moment, are pushed forward without intermission until the work capitulates.

480. Whilst the first parallel is still in an incomplete state, boyaux are commenced to lead from it to gain the position of the *Second Parallel*, which is laid out parallel to the first, and rather less than three hundred yards from it; so that it may be still under the protection of the first, whilst in an incomplete state, should the garrison attempt a sortie against it. The object of this parallel is to protect the approaches as they are pushed forward upon the salients. The same principle governs all the approaches: that is, they must be protected by a force superior to any that can be brought against them, and, in order that they may be succored in time, this force must be nearer than the garrison to the workmen employed in the trenches.

481. The construction of the second parallel differs from that of the first, owing to the exposed state of the workmen to the grape shot of the work. To place the men under cover, as speedily as possible, the line of the parallel is marked out, by placing gabions side by side, and when these gabions are filled, they afford a protection from grape shot.

482. With regard to the enfilading batteries, it is a disputed point whether they should be erected near the first or the second parallel. If the fire of the work attacked, is very warm and destructive, it may be necessary to place the batteries near the first parallel, to silence the fire of the work before the approaches can be pushed farther; but their effect, at this distance, is far less certain than at the second parallel, where every shot can be made to tell.

483. Whatever may be the place of the batte-

ries, their direction will be perpendicular to the face enfiladed. The batteries will contain cannon, howitzers, and mortars. The cannon destroy the guns and their traverses; the howitzers annoy the covered-ways; and the mortars throw shells into any part of the work which cannot otherwise be reached.

484. The approaches are carried forward from the second parallel, so soon as the fire of the place is silenced; but here the musket soon comes into play, a weapon of a more certain aim than cannon, and therefore more destructive to the workmen. The approaches are now given over to the engineer troops, termed *Sappers*, who carry forward the trench, termed a *Sap*, slowly, but with constant progress day and night. The *sappers* advance the end of the trench, working on their knees, and shielding themselves in front from the enemy's fire, by a large gabion stuffed with fascines, or wool, termed a *Sap-Roller*, which is rolled forward as they gradually advance.

485. When the boyaux are completed to within sixty yards of the most advanced salients of the work, the *Third Parallel* is commenced; the precaution having been taken, however, to place *Half Parallels*, between the second and third, to protect the approaches until the third is completed.

486. At the position of the third parallel, the besiegers have arrived on the immediate ground of the work attacked. Here the struggle begins to assume an attitude of equality. The attack loses its advantage of enveloping; it presents a front nearly the same as that of the defence; and shortly it becomes itself the enveloped; and then, if the resources of the garrison have not been entirely exhausted, each day will show but slight progress

13*

on the part of the besiegers, who are confined to their trenches, and exposed to all the disadvantages of a commanded and enveloped position.

487. After the completion of the third parallel, measures are taken to drive the garrison from the covered-ways, so that the breach batteries may be erected. This may be done in two ways; either by still proceeding by gradual approaches, or else an attack by storm may be made on the covered way, and whilst this action is going on, the sappers establish themselves along the crest of the glacis. The first method is slow, but certain, and accompanied with, comparatively speaking, but little loss of life. The second is rapid and more brilliant, but attended with great destruction of life, even in the most favorable cases, and is moreover seldom successful.

488. All open assaults of permanent works are attended with immense loss of life, and ought never to succeed where a garrison does its duty even with ordinary vigor. This is a maxim justified by the results of every attempt of this character on record; and it should never be lost sight of by the commanding officer of the siege. Nothing but a case of the most urgent necessity, where a day gained may decide the fate of the besiegers themselves, should cover from obloquy any officer, whatever success may crown his order, who wantonly sheds the blood of brave men to attain an object, which a few hours' delay would place within his reach, without perhaps the loss of a man.

489. To attack the covered way by storm, *Stone Mortar Batteries* are erected in front of the third parallel, for the purpose of throwing showers of stone into the covered-ways. A detachment of chosen troops is stationed in the third parallel, to dé-

bouche from it, at a given signal, and rush into the covered ways. The sappers are also in readiness, with their implements, to make the required lodgment on the glacis. When everything is prepared, a powerful fire is opened from the mortar batteries, and from all others, whose fire can reach the covered-way, to drive the besieged from it, and from their other defences near it. This shower of projectiles ceases at a concerted signal, and the men composing the detachment rush from the parallel, and throw themselves into the covered-way, driving everything before them, and availing themselves of every defensible point in order to prevent the besieged from sallying out, until the sappers, who follow close on them, have had time to construct a sap within six yards of the crest of the glacis, around the salient place of arms of the demi-lune covered-way, into which they can retire for shelter from the covered-way.

490. In the attack by gradual approaches, the sappers push forward the trench from the third parallel, under the protection of the fire from the stone mortar batteries, proceeding directly on the salient of the covered-way, and when they have arrived at thirty yards from it, they extend the sap fifteen or twenty yards to the right and left, so as to embrace these salients, and throw up a mound of earth about ten feet high, from the top of which they can obtain a plunging fire into the covered-way, and thus prevent the besieged from occupying it. This mound is termed the *Trench Cavalier*.

491. When the besieged are effectually driven from the covered-way, the sappers push forward the sap to within six yards of the crest of the glacis; and they make a trench entirely around the covered-way, which is termed *Crowning the Covered-Way*

After the covered-way is crowned, breach batteries are erected around the salient places of arms, and from these positions breaches are made in the face of the demi-lune, and in the bastion faces.

492. The besiegers now begin their operations to get at the breach, which is done by forming an underground gallery of frame-work and boards, leading to the bottom of the ditch; this is termed the *Descent of the Ditch*. From the bottom of this descent a trench is made, by sap, across the ditch, and up the slope of the breach to its top, where a trench encircling the top of the breach is formed; these operations are termed the *Passage of the Ditch*, and the *Lodgment of the Breach*.

493. In some cases the breach is carried by assault, but the same objection is applicable here as in the attack of the covered way by storm. It should only be resorted to when the besieged show, by their efforts, that the lodgment cannot be otherwise effected.

494. If the demi-lune is provided with a redoubt, this work must be taken before the bastion can be carried, because it has a reverse fire on the breach from its flanks. A breach battery will therefore have to be erected in the demi-lune against the redoubt, and when the breach is practicable, it may be assaulted at the same time as the bastion breach.

495. Similar operations will have to be made against the interior retrenchments, in the bastion. Finally, at the breach in the last work the garrison must capitulate, or undergo, according to the custom of war, the fate of those who are carried by storm.

496. DEFENCE. The measures for the defence, although for the most part prepared beforehand, will in some degree be subordinate to those of the attack. The fortifications are here supposed in a

complete state, and supplied with all the necessary provisions and munitions of war for a full garrison.

497. So soon as any indications of demonstrations against the work are seen, everything on the exterior, within cannon range, which might afford a shelter to the enemy, must be removed. One gun at least, of long range, is placed in barbette on each salient of the enceinte and demi-lunes; and at least two guns, loaded with case-shot, are placed in embrasure on each flank of the enceinte. These are simply measures of precaution to guard against a surprise, and to prevent reconnoitring bodies from approaching the work.

498. When the investment takes place, the garrison will resort to every expedient of open force and stratagem to cut off the enemy's reconnoitring parties; and, finally, when hemmed in by the superior forces of the besieging army, they will still watch every opportunity for annoying the enemy, by destroying his munitions, &c., without, however, jeoparding themselves, for they are now supposed beyond the reach of succors, and every life lost greatly increases the disproportion between their resources and those of the enemy.

499. When all the preparations for opening the trenches are completed, the garrison will bring forward all its disposable artillery, and place it, in barbette, along the point of attack, this point having been ascertained by the movements of the enemy's troops, the establishment of his parks, depots, &c. Every night, about the presumed time for opening the trenches, fire-balls will be thrown out, to discover the enemy's movements; and when he commences his labors, a heavy fire will be opened on his laborers and troops, at the same moment from every point, and it will be kept up without intermis-

sion for some hour. This is the moment that a select detachment of the garrison will sally out from the collateral works, and at a given signal the fire will cease, to allow them to charge the enemy's flank. If this sortie succeeds, it should be vigorously followed up; the workmen are dispersed, and during the confusion resulting from this, the detachment should, if there is the slightest prospect of success, endeavor to penetrate to the enemy's parks, and destroy everything in their way. This is the only moment that a vigorous sortie can be made with any success. The parallels once established, the odds become too great against the garrison to justify another attempt, except great remissness is observed on the part of the enemy.

500. The guns are withdrawn from the barbettes after the first night, and placed in embrasure on the most suitable points to retard the approaches; they are also covered in flank by traverses. A fire, mostly of ricochet, is kept up on all the works of the enemy, at regular intervals, until he has advanced within the range of grape and musketry, when both of these projectiles are resorted to; the artillery being served with the greatest coolness, and the best marksmen with muskets or rifles, being stationed in the covered-ways.

501. This system is persevered in, until the enemy gets on the glacis, or the immediate ground of the work. Then commences a system of *petite-guerre*, in which all means are taken to retard the work; sorties of a few picked men are continually made, to bayonet the sappers, and by throwing bags of powder, with slow-matches attached to them, against the sap-rollers, to blow them and the sapper up.

502. Finally, the covered-way is vigorously defended inch by inch, if attacked by storm, the troops

retreating from it under the protection of the fire of the works in its rear.

503. The defence of the breaches will chiefly depend on the measures of the attack; if these are by gradual approaches, the garrison will make frequent sorties from the adjacent works, in small bodies, on the passage across the ditch, whilst others attack the lodgment on the breach in front. But if the besiegers make their preparations to carry the breach by storm, the besieged should closely calculate the chances of opposing with the bayonet this attack. It is true that the military code, as generally received among nations, prescribes that the garrison should not accept terms of capitulation until they have sustained at least three assaults of the breach. But neither duty nor honor requires a brave man to sacrifice himself, when, all prospect of succor or of retreat being shut out, he finds himself in position, face to face, with ten to one against him, and entirely at the mercy of his enemy in case of defeat.

504. A breach can only be defended with a certainty of success, and without jeoparding the lives of the entire garrison, when a redoubt or interior retrenchment is in its rear, under the cover of whose fire the troops, placed at the breach to watch the enemy's movements, and delay his progress, can retreat with safety. When this measure of security is provided, the troops at the breach should use every human means, short of attacking with the bayonet, to prevent the enemy from advancing, and they must not retire before there is an appearance of imminent danger to the point of safety, from the enemy entering it pe'l-mell with the retreating detachment.

505. In a general summary of the ordinary march of the attack and defence, and the applica-

tion of the principles of permanent fortification, no allusion has been made to accessory measures of defence, which often furnish both parties with the most powerful resources, as *mines*, the uses of *water, &c.;* since these measures are not of universal application, owing to their requiring suitable localities for their employment; and they would, moreover, require explanations and details, which none but the professional engineer would probably understand, and which would offer no interest to any other.

506. *Uses of permanent works.* The subject of national defence is one which presents itself with such strong claims to the careful consideration, not only of the statesman and soldier, but of every private citizen, as all have the deepest interests at stake, in the settlement of so momentous a question as the safety of the State, that a few words seemed called for on the part which permanent works play in the military organization of a frontier; and the relations subsisting between their action and that of other means of defence.

A thorough discussion of this subject would embrace too wide a field to be brought within the present scope of the writer; for to do full justice to it, he would be obliged to enter into the development of the principles of other branches of the military art in some respects foreign to the purposes of this essay. But there are a few reflections of too striking a character to be suppressed, and which the events recorded, not only in the history of foreign nations, but in that of our own country, must bring forcibly home to the breast of every thinking person.

To defend the utility, the indispensable necessity of the military organization of a frontier with per-

157

manent works, were to cite the experience of every
people, of every age, who have been exposed to the
disasters of invasion, whether upon their land or
maritime frontier. Poland, owing to the want of
such an organization, fell a victim to the greatest
political crime of modern times. Spain had well
nigh been ensnared in an insidious attempt against
her existence as an independent nation, of as dark
a dye as the dismemberment of Poland, when the
heroic resistance of Saragossa, and a few other
fortified places, gave her people time to recover
from their first surprise, and enabled them to rally
under the protection of their strongholds, and or-
ganize that system of determined resistance, that
"war to the knife," which at length freed their
soil from the pollution of a foreign master's foot-
steps. France saw her naval power annihilated,
and her commercial marine literally swept from the
seas, by the loss of a few naval pitched battles;
and whilst the fleets of her enemy rode in triumph
at her very threshold, slept on in unbroken security, under the guns of her sea-board defences. At
a subsequent period, when, overwhelmed by the
united forces of Europe, her hitherto victorious
armies were driven within their own territory, it
is the opinion of able military men, that a few
strongholds on the flank of the enemy would have
enabled her great Captain, who contended with his
usual genius against such unequal odds, to have
retrieved her fortunes, whilst that enemy rushed on
to seize her open unprotected capital, and afterwards trembled in its possession at the thought of
a reaction in the people.

No intelligent person, it is presumed, could be
found, in the present advanced stage of military
science, to advocate a system of defence with ac-
14

tive forces alone, whether land or naval. The
perishable nature of such armaments, the casualties
to which they are exposed, the uncertainty of the
issue of pitched battles, all point to some other
means of defence, which, by prolonging the contest
on one or more points, will increase the chances of
retrieving any mishaps. To defend an open frontier of any nature, without the aid of permanent
works, requires the display of a large moveable
military force, whose ultimate expense, long experience has but too amply proved, increases in a rapid proportion with the undisciplined character of
the troops. This is the opinion of military men of
all nations; and the testimony of our generals,
whether of the militia, or of the regular army, goes
to show; that whatever reliance may be placed on
the valor and patriotism of our militia in times of
emergency, still it is necessarily the most expensive
force that can be brought into the field against an
enemy, owing to the losses which are necessarily
incurred by the employment of men totally unac-
quainted with the economy of a regularly organized
army. This being the case, and the nature of our
political institutions being such as to render a resort
to a large standing army dangerous to their existence, it behooves us to devise some means by which
the smallest regular force may be called for in defence of the State, and in which the militia may be
employed, not only in the most efficient manner for
the defence, but also most economically.

The best means, it seems to the writer, by which
this can be effected, consists in a judicious organization of the frontier, with permanent works of such
strength as each particular site may require. The
defence of these works may be safely left to garrisons principally of militia; and as this arm of our

national defence is composed of the most valuable members of society, this kind of service will be most appropriately intrusted to it, as it is less onerous to the individual than that of the field, and is, moreover, attended with less destruction of life, both from the diseases incident to the exposure of the camp and the casualties of pitched battles.

As to the class of permanent works which would be required for an efficient organization of our frontier, the writer does not feel himself called on to give an opinion, as this is a point which ought to be settled alone by a board of competent engineer officers. Without permanent defences, both our land and sea-board frontier would be left open, not only to the temporary inroads of an enemy's armies and fleets, but, as was seen during our last war with England, positions could be selected, and permanently occupied by him during the war, from which our entire coast might be kept in a state of continued alarm, whilst great detriment might be caused to our coasting trade, and to the line of the sea-board, from occasional marauding parties and small cruisers. With permanent works of a proper character at suitable points, the most of these evils would be obviated; our harbors would be secured, and our large roadsteads, with even the extensive estuaries for which our coast is remarkable, could be effectually closed against an enemy's squadrons. These strongholds would serve as places of resort for our own vessels of war, when in less strength than those of the enemy, where they could lie in security, and watch for a favorable moment of action. They would serve as covering points for our fleets, in event of any disaster happening, either from battle or from tempests. They would form the natural rallying points for floating batteries, moved by steam, by means of which the enemy would at all times be kept on the alert, and his posi tion at any point far beyond the range of the guns of the work, would be rendered insecure, and in most cases, untenable, except at a great risk. In our land operations, these fortified points would play anything but a passive part, if properly combined with moveable forces. In the hands of a skilful general, their part, on the contrary, would be eminently active. They might be made to cover, not only their own garrisons, but large bodies of troops which might take up an unassailable position under their guns, and be in readiness at all times to oppose the enemy in front, if of equal force, or to attack his flank or rear, if he attempted to treat them with neglect. They might be made to serve as points of safety, upon which the garrisons of weaker works could retreat in case of necessity, or from which they could obtain succor if strongly pressed by a superior force. It is in this way that permanent works become truly formidable to an enemy, and enable us to guard distant points beyond the range of their cannon, without placing a man, or a gun, for the immediate defence of those points.

NOTE A.

Manner of determining the proportion between the terre-plein of a Square Redoubt, the development of its interior crest, and the size of its garrison.

Fig. A.

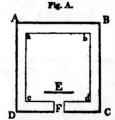

Let A B C D (Fig. A.) be the line of the interior crest; a b c d that of the foot of the banquette slope; F the outlet through the parapet; and E the interior traverse.

Representing by x, the number of yards in the side A B, the side a b will be equal to x diminished by twice the distance between A B and a b, which distance may be taken on an average at 9 yards; the area of the square b c, or of the terre-plein, will then be represented by $(x-9)^2$.

Let the following notation be adopted:—

x, the side of the square A B.

y, the number of the garrison.

r, the reserve taken from the garrison.

n, the number of ranks on the banquette for the defence.

s, the area of the terre-plein occupied by a barbette in the salient.

14*

s', the area occupied on the terre-plein by the powder-magazine.

s'', the area occupied by the traverse, and the passage in its rear.

l, the number of yards on the interior crest for a barbette in the salient.

l', the width of the outlet F in yards.

Now, as the area allowed for each man is one and a half square yards, we shall obtain the following equation, to represent the relation between the terre-plein, the garrison, &c.

$$(s-9)^2 = 1,50\,y + s + s' + s''; \ldots \quad (1)$$

this is termed *the equation of the interior space*.

As each man occupies one lineal yard along the interior crest, we obtain also,

$$4s = \frac{y-r}{2} + l + l'; \ldots \ldots \quad (2)$$

which is termed *the equation of defence*, as it expresses the relation between the development of the interior crest, the remainder of the garrison after taking out the reserve, the number of ranks for the defence, and the length of the interior crest required for the cannon in barbette, and for the outlet.

To show the application of the equations (1) and (2), let it be required to find the side of a redoubt, and the number of its garrison, which shall be defended by two ranks on the banquette, after taking out a reserve of one-third of the whole number, and have a barbette in each salient.

By a calculation, easily made, it can be shown, that each barbette will occupy about 75 square yards of the terre-plein; a powder magazine for four guns, 20 square yards; a traverse of earth, with the passage between it and the foot of the banquette, about 180 square yards; or, if of timber, about 50 square yards; the portion of the interior crest for each barbette will be nearly 18 lineal yards; and that for the passage about 4 lineal yards.

Taking Eq. (2), and making the substitutions required by the conditions of the Prob. we obtain,

$$4z = \frac{y - \frac{1}{2}y}{2} + 4 + 72;$$

and from it,

$$y = 12z - 228.$$

Substituting this value of y in Eq. (1), and placing for s, s', s'', their values, we have

$$(z - 9)^2 = 18z - 342 + 300 + 20 + 180;$$

or,

$$(z - 9)^2 = 18z + 158;$$

from which, by solving the equation,

$$z = 38 \text{ yards};$$

consequently $y = 228$ men;

and $r = 76$ men.

NOTE B.

Manner of equalizing the Excavation of the Ditch, and the Embankment of the Parapet.

Fig. B.

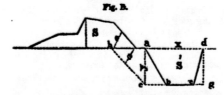

Let the following notation be adopted, Fig. B.

V, Volume of the embankment.

S, Surface of its profile.

l, Line described by the centre of gravity of S in generating the embankment.

V′, S′, and *l*′, corresponding values of the ditch.

Now, from the centre-baryc principle, we have

$$V = S\, l; \quad . \; . \; (1), \text{ and } V' = S'\, l'; \; . \; . \; (2).$$

But as earth, when freshly thrown up, occupies a greater volume than in its natural state, if this increase be represented by the fraction $\frac{1}{m}$, we shall have to represent this condition

$$V = V' + \frac{1}{m} V'; \quad . \; . \; . \; . \; (3)$$

and eliminating V and V′, by means of these three equations, there results

$$S' = S \frac{l}{l'} \left(\frac{m}{m+1} \right); \quad . \; . \; . \; (4)$$

or the value of the surface of the profile of the ditch in known quantities.

Representing now by

x, the width of the ditch $=$ a d;

y, its depth $=$ a e;

a, the angle of the natural slope of the earth with the ground $=$ a h e.

We obtain

$$a\,h = y\ Cot.\ a;$$

and for the bases of the slopes of the scarp and counterscarp,

$$e\,b = \tfrac{1}{3}\,a\,h = \tfrac{1}{3}\,y\ Cot.\ a;\ \text{and}\ c\,g = \tfrac{1}{3}\,a\,h = \tfrac{1}{3}\,y\ Cot.\ a.$$

we then obtain for the area of the trapezoid a b c d, which is S', by subtracting the surfaces of the triangles a e b, and c g d, from the rectangle a g,

$$S' = x\,y - (\tfrac{1}{3}\,y^2\ Cot.\ a + \tfrac{1}{3}\,y^2\ Cot.\ a);$$

or, $\quad S' = x\,y - \tfrac{5}{18}\,y^2\ Cot.\ a;\ \cdot\ \cdot\ \cdot\ (5)$

an equation from which either x or y may be obtained, by assuming either the width or the depth. But as x has certain limits, from the nature of the Prob., we will solve Eq. (5) with respect to y, and will obtain,

$$y = \tfrac{1}{2}\ Tan.\ a\ (x - \sqrt{x^2 - \tfrac{1}{2}\,s'\ Cot.\ a,})\ .\ .\ (6)$$

We observe here, in the first place, that the radical expression admits only the minus sign before it, because x and y are decreasing functions of each other; that x^2 cannot be less than $\tfrac{1}{2}\,S'\ Cot.\ a$, otherwise the expression will become imaginary; and when it is equal to it, the profile of the ditch becomes a triangle, so that the minima limits of x will be,

$$x = \sqrt{\tfrac{1}{2}\,S'\ Cot.\ a};\ \text{and}\ x = 12\ \text{feet};\ (\text{Art. 39.})$$

and the maximum value will be found by multiplying the height of the interior crest by the denominator of the fraction which represents the superior slope, and subtracting from this result the horizonta. distance between the interior crest, and the crest of the scarp. (Art. 34.)

Any quantity, therefore, which is greater than the minima limits, and less than the maximum, will satisfy the conditions of the Prob., if it gives for a result y between 6 and 12 feet. (Art. 39.)

But should the value of y not fall between these limits, then we shall be obliged to change the form of S; and consequently find a new value of S′; making it greater or smaller, as the case may require.

To show the manner of applying this formula to practice, let it be required to find the dimensions of the ditch of a square redoubt from the following data; the command of the interior crest is 8 feet; the thickness of the parapet 9 feet; the superior slope 1-6th; the angle of the natural slope 45°; and the tread of the banquette 4 feet.

Taking, in the first place, Eq. (4),

$$S' = S \frac{l}{l'} \left(\frac{m}{m+1} \right)$$

a very simple calculation will show that $\frac{l}{l'}$ will be very nearly represented by the fraction $\frac{3}{4}$, for redoubts between 20 and 40 yards of a side, measured along the interior crest, l' being the middle line of the top of a ditch, which is a mean between the least and greatest limits. The value of $\frac{1}{m}$ is, in ordinary earth, about $\frac{1}{8}$, and varies generally between $\frac{1}{6}$ and $\frac{1}{12}$, so that, by substituting these values in the Eq., we have

$$S' = \frac{3}{4} \left(\frac{8}{8+1} \right) S = \frac{2}{3} S;$$

and the value of S, calculated from the data, being 122 square feet, we have

$$S' = 81, \text{ square feet nearly };$$

substituting this value of S' in Eq. (6), we obtain

$$y = \frac{a}{c}\,(x - \sqrt{x^2 - 189});$$

from which we see that $x^2 = 189$, gives $x = 13$ feet, therefore the quantity assumed for x must be greater than this; if then, we assume $x = 15$ feet, and substitute it in this formula, we obtain

$$y = \frac{a}{c}\,(15 - \sqrt{225 - 189});$$

or $\qquad y = \frac{a}{c}\,(15 - 6) = 7.7$ feet;

which satisfies the required conditions.

It may be added, that with this width of ditch, the line of fire passes 2.6 feet above the counterscarp crest.

In the foregoing calculations, no allowance has been made for the volumes of the barbettes; and the traverse when of earth. To make this allowance, Eqs. (3) and (4) will have to undergo a suitable modification, as follows :—

The cubic contents of each barbette, in a salient, is nearly 140 yards; and that of the traverse about .70 yards. If, then, the total cubic contents of all the barbettes, and the traverse, be represented by V'', a given quantity, Eq. (3) will become

$$V + V'' = V' + \frac{1}{m}\,V' \quad . \quad . \quad . \quad \text{(X)};$$

and

$$S\,l + V'' = S'\,l' + \frac{1}{m}\,S'\,l', \quad . \quad . \quad . \quad \text{(Y)};$$

Now, as V'' is a given quantity, it can be represented by $S''\,l$, in which S'' is found by dividing V'' by l; making this substitution in Eq. (Y), we obtain

$$S' = (S + S'')\,\frac{l}{l'}\,\left(\frac{m}{m+1}\right) \quad . \quad . \quad . \quad \text{(Z)}$$

for the modified value of S′ Eq. (4), to suit this case. The operations for finding x and y, Eq. (6) are the same as already shown.

The calculations here given suppose the plane of site sensibly horizontal, and the interior crest parallel to it; when this is not so, as, for example, in a defiladed work, the volumes of the parapet and ditch will have to be calculated for each face separately.

The method of doing this, where the site is very irregular, consists in making an unequal number of parallel profiles, on each face, at equal distances from each other, and finding the area of each pro file, and then using the following notation and for mula,

·et s', s'', s''', s^{IV}, ... s^{n+1} , represent the areas of the successive profiles, their entire num ber being $n + 1$;

l, the distance between the profiles;

v, the volume between the extreme profiles; then

$$v = \frac{l}{3}\left(s' + 4s'' + 2s''' + 4s^{IV} + 2s^{V} \ldots 4s^{n} + s^{n+1}\right).$$

In other cases, where the site is not very irregular, a mean profile may be found, and the Eq. (Z) be used.

It is usually best, since the dimensions of the ditch cannot be uniform throughout, to adopt a uniform depth, and to vary the width as circumstances may require.

RECENT PUBLICATIONS

OF

JOHN WILEY.

56 WALKER ST., N.Y.

———

L

Thoughts, Feelings, and Fancies.

By C. N. BOVEE.

One vol. 12mo., fancy cloth, bevel boards, gilt top, $1 25

From the Evangelist.

"Beautiful in conception and terse in expression, the fruits of an extensive observation, and a keen sagacity. The volume as a whole is a highly suggestive one, abounding in germs of thought, and embodying the results of much and careful reflection. Such a volume, as the product of a single mind, is truly a marvel."

From the Christian Freeman.

"This we regard as one of the richest gems of the season. It clearly proves the author to be a healthy, vigorous and original thinker, and we most heartily recommend it to every intelligent reader. No page can be read without entertainment and profit."

From the Daily Pennsylvanian.

"The perfume from a garden of reading, and the seed of ripened thought. It is distinguished by good sense and careful observation."

From the Observer.

"Abounding in striking thoughts on an almost endless variety of subjects, in which the author displays much general reading and thinking."

From the Christian Intelligencer.

" This is one of the very best parlor-books that has met our eye in many a day. It equals, if it does not excel, Lacon."

II.

THE STORY OF A POCKET BIBLE.

NEW EDITION.

WITH CORRECTIONS AND ADDITIONS.

Illustrated with numerous Plates.

One vol., 12mo., $1.

" It vividly and powerfully portrays the varied experience of the soul under the influence of divine truth, combining with the interest of the novel the pungency of a religious tract, and illustrations of the power of the Bible, which must affect the most careless and indifferent. There is a great variety of scene and character alike truthfully and tastefully drawn. We heartily commend it as a work of absorbing interest, and eminently calculated to do good."—*Evangelist.*

" It will be equally valuable for family reading, and for Sabbath-school and district-school libraries. We trust that it will be widely circulated among the young."—*Independent.*

" Its spirit is good and earnest, and must commend itself to every one who recognises in literature not merely a pleasant intellectual entertainment, but a useful medium for wholesome discipline and moral culture."—*New Yorker.*

" An ingenious and interesting, as well as very instructive book, beautifully published, in which the various characters into whose hands this Bible falls are exhibited, with such a variety of incident and illustration as to make a strong impression. It is a capital book."—*Observer.*

III.
JAUFRY THE KNIGHT AND THE FAIR BRUNISSENDE.

A TALE OF THE TIMES OF KING ARTHUR.

Translated from the French version of Mary Lafon, by ALFRED ELWES. Illustrated with Engravings. 1 vol. 8vo., $1.

From the Courier and Enquirer.
"It is a piquant, fanciful, and exceedingly charming tale of knightly romance, abounding in poetry and redolent of chivalry through and through. The poetic rhythm of the original is still retained, and so effectively does it blend with the strange adventures of the story that even the most practical and prosaic reader of the first page will find it very hard to lay down the book until he finishes the last."

From the Evening Post.
"The story is full of invention; the incidents, particularly the combats, are related with such narrative power, that the reader will not wonder that works of this kind should have formed the amusement of the closet six hundred years ago."

IV.
THE ELEMENTS OF DRAWING.

In Three Letters to Beginners,

BY JOHN RUSKIN, M.A.,

Author of "Modern Painters," "Seven Lamps of Architecture," &c., &c.

LETTER I. On First Practice.
II. Sketching from Nature.
III. On Color and Composition.
APPENDIX—Things to be Studied.
1 vol. 12mo, with Fifty Illustrations. Price $1.

V.

RUSKIN'S COMPLETE WORKS.

Uniform in Size and Binding.

Nine vols. 12mo. Dark cloth, $11 50.

CONSISTING OF

L

MODERN PAINTERS. Four vols. 12mo., full dark cloth.
$5 50.

II.

THE SEVEN LAMPS OF ARCHITECTURE, with fourteen
etchings by the Author. 1 vol. 12mo., full dark cloth, $1 25

III.

THE STONES OF VENICE. The Foundations. 1 vol. 12mo.,
with numerous wood engravings, full dark cloth, $2.

IV

PRE-RAPHAELITISM, AND NOTES ON THE CONSTRUC-
TION OF SHEEP-FOLDS. 1 vol. 12mo., full dark cloth,
50 cents.

V.

LECTURES ON ARCHITECTURE AND PAINTING, with
fifteen illustrations on tinted paper. 1 vol. 12mo., full dark
cloth, $1 25.

VL

THE ELEMENTS OF DRAWING. In Three Letters to Be-
ginners. 1 vol. 12mo., full dark cloth, $1.

"It is needless to criticise or commend the works of Ruskin.
They have an individuality so distinctly marked that the reader
receives them as the views of a master who has become absorbed
in his theme. The lines of art are embellished with all the graces
of an elegant literature, and a work produced that is read with
profit by every cultivated mind."—*N. Y. Observer.*

LaVergne, TN USA
01 December 2009
165577LV00009B/180/A